A Curious Student's Guide to the Book of Exodus

A Curious Student's Guide to the Book of Exodus

Enduring Life Lessons
for the Twenty-First Century

REUVEN TRAVIS

WIPF & STOCK · Eugene, Oregon

A CURIOUS STUDENT'S GUIDE TO THE BOOK OF EXODUS
Enduring Life Lessons for the Twenty-First Century

Wipf & Stock
An Imprint of Wipf and Stock Publishers
199 W. 8th Ave., Suite 3
Eugene, OR 97401

www.wipfandstock.com

PAPERBACK ISBN: 978-1-7252-7195-1
HARDCOVER ISBN: 978-1-7252-7196-8
EBOOK ISBN: 978-1-7252-7197-5

06/18/21

Original illustrations by Eli Portman.

In Honor of my Newest Grandchild
Teo "Teddy" Levine

The cure for boredom is curiosity.
There is no cure for curiosity.

—Dorothy Parker

Contents

CONTENTS

Acknowledgements

I would like to thank my dear friend and colleague Lisa Marks for the many hours she spent looking over the various drafts of this book that I shared with her. Her comments and suggestions were invaluable and in the end made this a better book.

So, too, I want to thank the fine folks at Wipf & Stock for the confidence they have shown in me by agreeing to publish this second *Curious Student's Guide*. With a little patience on their part (and, of course, with continued help from God), I hope to complete in the not-so-distant future a multi-volume set of life lessons for curious students of the Bible.

Rabbi Reuven Travis

Preface for Parents and Educators

The fact you have purchased this book demonstrates that you recognize the importance of teaching Exodus to your children or students in a manner that engages and challenges them. However, it is worth considering whether these children also see the value in studying Exodus in depth. They may feel that having learned about the Passover holiday and attended seder after seder over the years, they already know what they need to know about Exodus.

Let's try to give a broader context and rationale for studying Exodus.

Children, especially those who attend a Jewish school (whether a day school or a synagogue school) can readily understand why they spend so much time learning Genesis. Genesis teaches us about the creation of the world and God's continued involvement with it. It details the origins of the Jewish people and their special covenant with God. Genesis is full of tales that children can appreciate: stories of good and bad characters, stories of God dealing directly with the world, stories about families. These are precisely the types of stories children can relate to and can learn with relative ease.

For children, Exodus is arguably both more familiar and more obscure.

The central narrative of Exodus is, of course, familiar to anyone, adult or child, who has attended a Passover seder. And while it is difficult to speak of "contempt" when discussing the study of the Bible, the old adage about familiarity breeding it holds some truth here.

The remoteness of Exodus, at least from a child's perspective, derives from the complexity of the topics it addresses, such as slavery, free will (or lack thereof), and idolatry. Add to this the fact that the second half of the book details the construction of the tabernacle, at times with mind-numbing detail, and we have a text that can leave children less than enthralled.

This is unfortunate, because the book of Exodus has had, and continues to have, a larger and more significant impact on our society than any other of the five books of the Pentateuch. This is true for Jews and Christians alike, and while this notion will likely be difficult for your children or students to grasp, your having this perspective might help you to engender in them greater enthusiasm for reading through this book with you.

Let's start with the world of entertainment. There are few more iconic images in cinematic history than that of Charlton Heston as Moses splitting the sea in Cecil B. Demille's 1956 movie classic *The Ten Commandments*. Consider, too, DreamWorks's 1998 animated musical drama *The Prince of Egypt*. Its worldwide box office gross exceeded two hundred million dollars, and it still ranks as one of the top-grossing non-Disney animated films of all time.

Then there is the impact of Exodus on our legal system. Over the years, there have been multiple court battles involving public displays of the Ten Commandments and whether such displays violate the Establishment Clause of the U.S. Constitution, which prohibits the government from making any law "respecting an establishment of religion." This issue of "separation of church and state," as Thomas Jefferson famously described it, was resolved in a creative manner by the courts. The Ten Commandments can be publicly displayed in government buildings, such as court houses, if they are part of a larger historical presentation of sources that undergird our legal system, such as the Magna Carta and the U.S. Constitution.[1] Clearly, the book of Exodus, or at least its legal sections, is seen as an integral part of our legal tradition.

1. In its 2005 decision *McCreary County v. ACLU*, the U.S. Supreme Court

Most important of all is the question of how the book of Exodus has shaped the foundations and development of our country.

The earliest the English settlers to arrive in the New World, the men and women who founded Jamestown in 1607, likened themselves to Moses and the Israelites who fled Egypt.[2] Even more significant is the example of the Pilgrims, who set sail on the Mayflower in September 1620 in search of a place in which they could practice their religion free of persecution. It is well known that they saw themselves as reliving the Exodus saga. Here is how Bruce Feiler, the author of *America's Prophet: How the Story of Moses Shaped America*, describes the mindset of the Pilgrims:

> Everything the Pilgrims had done for two decades was designed to fulfill their dream of creating God's New Israel. When they first left England for Holland in 1608, they described themselves as the chosen people, casting off the yoke of their pharaoh, King James. A dozen years later, when they embarked on a grander exodus, to America, their leader, William Bradford, proclaimed their mission to be as vital as that of "Moses and the Israelites when they went out of Egypt." And when, after sixty-six days on the Atlantic, they finally arrived at Cape Cod, they were brought to their knees in gratitude for safe passage through their own Red Sea.[3]

In a very real sense, the Pilgrims thought of their lives and experiences as literal reenactments of the biblical drama set forth in the book of Exodus. To put it differently, the Pilgrims "saw themselves as the children of Israel; America was their Promised Land;

---

ruled five to four that the Ten Commandments could not be displayed in court buildings or on government property. However, the justices held that the biblical laws could be displayed in a historical context, as they are in a frieze in the Supreme Court building. Notably, the first four commandments, which have to do with honoring God and the Sabbath, were obscured by the artist who designed the frieze.

2. Feiler, *America's Prophet*, 8.

3. Feiler, *America's Prophet*, 8.

the Atlantic Ocean their Red Sea; the Kings of England were the Egyptian pharaohs; the American Indians the Canaanites."[4]

This perspective did not end with the early settlers of America. It was also present in the thoughts and writings of our founding fathers. For instance, during the American Revolution, Thomas Paine's *Common Sense*, published in January 1776, had a profound impact on the colonists and helped inflame their desire for independence. In this work, Paine described King George III as the "sullen tempered pharaoh of England." Perhaps the most famous example of the influence of Exodus on America's early leaders is a letter sent by George Washington after his election to the presidency to the members of Congregation Mickve Israel in Savannah, Georgia:[5]

> May the same wonder-working Deity, who long since delivered the Hebrews from their Egyptian oppressors, planted them in the promised land, whose providential agency has lately been conspicuous in establishing these United States as an independent nation, still continue to water them with the dews of heaven.[6]

The impact of the book of Exodus on the American psyche is not limited to the founding of our country. It was also manifest in one of America's most critical and challenging epochs, namely, the antebellum era. During this time, both enslaved people and enslavers used the Exodus narrative to form their respective identities and to define their purpose in America. Enslavers saw themselves as the New Israel, the "Redeemer Nation."[7] These Southerners believed that the social and economic systems they had crafted positioned them "to reach the pinnacle of perfection," and, like the ancient Israelites

---

4. Freund, "How the Exodus Story Created America."

5. Congregation Mickve Israel is one of the oldest synagogues in the United States. It was established in 1735 by a group of mostly Sephardic Jewish immigrants of Spanish-Portuguese extraction who arrived in the new colony from London in 1733.

6. Feiler, *America's Prophet*, 4.

7. Raboteau, *Fire in the Bones.*

who brought God's law into the world, these enslavers were ready "to carry liberty and the gospel around the globe."[8]

For the enslaved people themselves, the Exodus story was not just a Jewish story. It was their story, too, and in their version, enslavers were cast in the role of Pharaoh.[9] Exodus gave the enslaved people (or at least some of them) hope, for this biblical narrative showed that deliverance was possible. By appropriating the account of Exodus, the enslaved people did more than simply try to understand their situation and their past; they created for themselves a national identity and, equally important, a mythic past.[10]

Enslavers understood the potential power the book of Exodus could exert on the people they enslaved. More than understood— they feared the exodus narrative, so much that "English missionaries seeking to convert enslaved Africans toiling in Britain's Caribbean colonies around the beginning of the nineteenth century preached from Bibles that conveniently removed portions of the canonical text. They thought these sections, such as Exodus, the Book of Psalms, and the Book of Revelation, could instill in slaves a dangerous hope for freedom and dreams of equality."[11]

Exodus continues to resonate and influence readers today, as does the leadership model of Moses that is evident throughout the book. Examples of this influence abound, such as the Statue of Liberty carrying a tablet meant to evoke the image of Moses carrying tablets inscribed with the Ten Commandments. We know that wartime presidents, such as Woodrow Wilson, Franklin Roosevelt, and Lyndon Johnson, tapped into a Mosaic leadership model. Perhaps most famously, Martin Luther King Jr. likened himself to Moses on the night before he was killed.[12] More recently, both Hillary Clinton and Barack Obama placed themselves in the Mosaic tradition during their 2008 campaigns, to the point that Obama's rival John McCain released a video in which he mocked Obama

8. Raboteau, *Fire in the Bones*.

9. Kay, "Exodus and Racism."

10. Raboteau, *Fire in the Bones*, 128.

11. Zehavi, "19th-cent. Slave Bible."

12. Feiler, *America's Prophet*, 4.

for anointing himself "the One."[13] Even the image of baby Kal-El, who would grow up to be the world's protector as Superman, is reflective of baby Moses being pulled from his wicker basket.[14]

Adults can grasp and appreciate the importance of the book of Exodus and the impact it has had on so many aspects of their lives. The discussions and life lessons culled from Exodus set forth in the pages that follow are intended to help your children and students develop a similar appreciation of Exodus.

Maximizing the utility of this book as you share it with your children and students necessitates a few more observations.

When teaching children about the Bible, one must pick and choose among the Pentateuch's many lessons so as to emphasize those that young students can grasp and appreciate. In the case of a book like Genesis, deciding which stories to skip (such as those of Dinah and the encounter between Judah and Tamar) is relatively easy. When it comes to Exodus, however, this becomes a much more complicated task. For example, one cannot omit the story of the sin of the golden calf, but it must be presented with great delicacy and nuance for young readers.

Another challenge in teaching children the books of the Pentateuch is differentiating between the text itself and the accompanying biblical exegesis. This is particularly tricky in Jewish homes and schools where adults often turn to midrash (a form of biblical exegesis developed and employed by ancient Judaic authorities) as a tool for helping children better understand the biblical narrative. Midrash provides us with important insights into and backstories to the text, but students should never conflate it with the Bible itself. The biblical text is the text, and midrash is commentary on the text.

When using midrash to make the text more easily understood, whether in the classroom or in my home interacting with my own children, I have always been guided by the approach of Rabbi Moshe ben Nachman, the great biblical commentator from

13. Feiler, *America's Prophet*, 8.

14. Feiler, *America's Prophet*, 5. See also Kinnaird, "Moses and the Man of Steel."

the 1200s. In his famous disputation with the apostate Jew Pablo Christiani, Rabbi Moshe made this observation:

> We possess three genres of literature. The first is the Bible or Tanakh, and all of us believe in its words with a complete trust. The second is the Talmud, and it is an exposition of the commandments of the Torah, for the Torah contains 613 commandments. Not a single one of them is left unexplained by the Talmud. We believe in the Talmud with respect to its exposition of the commandments. The third type of book that we possess is the Midrash, and it is like sermons . . . concerning this collection, for one who believes it, good. For one who does not believe it, there is no harm . . . "[15]

I have never been one to insist that students see midrashic expositions as accurate, historical accounts, nor have I framed midrashic stories as mere parables. How a student chooses to see this literature is up to him or her. But what cannot be ignored or diminished are the important lessons the midrash offers us. Consider the following midrash, one of the best known on the book of Exodus.

When Moses argues with God and claims that he is not up to the task of bringing the Jewish people out of Egypt, he offers the following rationale: "Please, O Lord, I have never been a man of words, either in times past or now that You have spoken to Your servant; I am slow of speech and slow of tongue." The rabbinic tradition understands this to mean that Moses stuttered. But what was the cause of his stuttering? Most Jewish students are familiar with this midrashic explanation:

> [Why does Pharaoh wish to meet the baby Moses?] Some said to kill him, and some said to burn him. And Jethro was sitting among them and said to them, "This child has no intent [to take the throne]. Rather, test him by bringing in a bowl [a piece of] gold and [a piece of burning] coal. If he outstretches his hand towards the gold, [surely] he has intent [to take the throne], and you

---

15. Nahmanides, *Disputation at Barcelona*, para. 39.

should kill him. And if he outstretches his hand towards the coal, he [surely] does not have intent [to take the throne], and he does not deserve the death penalty." They immediately brought the bowl before him [Moses], and he outstretched his hand to take the gold, and Gabriel came and pushed his [Moses's] hand, and he grabbed the coal. He then brought his hand along with the coal into his mouth and burned his tongue, and from this was made "slow of speech and slow of tongue" (Exod 4:10). (*Shemot Rabbah* 1:26)

It is worthwhile and enlightening for students to know this story of the burning coal, but it is critical that they recognize it as midrash and understand that it is not found in the text of Exodus itself. Therefore, throughout this book, when midrash is used to explain the text, it will be identified as such, or it will be referred to as "the rabbinic tradition."

In addition to understanding how and when midrash is used in this book, readers should also be familiar with the approach I employ for presenting and examining the central stories of Exodus. (This will be familiar if you have read my Genesis book.) In brief, I have opted not to use the system of chapters and verse numbers most students of the Bible are acquainted with. This division was first made in the Latin Bible in the thirteenth century, most likely by Stephen Langston.[16] Langston's system was employed in the concordances of the Vulgate, and this in turn gave Rabbi Isaac Nathan[17] the idea for the first Hebrew concordance. The citations in this concordance first give the number of the Vulgate chapter and then give the

16. Stephen Langton was an English cardinal of the Roman Catholic Church and Archbishop of Canterbury from 1207 to his death in 1228. The dispute between King John of England and Pope Innocent III over his election as archbishop was a major factor in the crisis that produced the Magna Carta in 1215.

17. Rabbi Isaac Nathan ben Kalonymus was a French Jewish philosopher who lived in the fourteenth and fifteenth centuries. In the introduction to his concordance, Rabbi Isaac wrote that he was completely ignorant of the Bible until his fifteenth year. Prior to that time, his studies had been restricted to the Talmud and religious philosophy.

number of the Masoretic[18] verse chapter, which remains to this day the standard format of the printed Hebrew Bible.

However, the printed format of the Hebrew Bible is not the one used for ritual purposes. As part of Jewish prayer services on the Sabbath, different portions of the Pentateuch are read each week.[19] These readings are commonly referred to as the weekly *parasha* or *sedra*. The starting and ending points of each parasha have nothing at all to do with Langston's system for organizing the Bible. Rather, they reflect the long-standing masoretic tradition.

Given my background and training as an Orthodox Jewish rabbi and educator, it made sense for me to organize this book according to these weekly parashas. It is a system I know well and am comfortable with. More important, these weekly readings, in my opinion, present a more logical flow for the major themes and stories of Exodus than do the chapter and verse numbers in common usage.[20]

Each chapter of this book will open with a brief overview and synopsis of the weekly Torah reading. Then will come a section I call "Life Lessons from This Week's Reading," which has the goal of helping young students think more deeply about the text read each week, as opposed to merely memorizing certain incidents from the narrative. Finally, there will be questions for students to think about as they begin to make the lessons from each week's reading their own.

All translations of biblical verses in this book are from *Tanakh: A New Translation of the Holy Scriptures according to the*

---

18. In rabbinic Judaism, the Masoretic Text is the authoritative Hebrew and Aramaic text of the Bible. It was copied, edited, and distributed primarily by a group of Jews known as the Masoretes between the seventh and tenth centuries CE.

19. There are fifty-four such weekly portions, which means that a double portion is read on some weeks.

20. Indeed, there are many chapter breaks that interrupt the logical flow of the narrative, which the masoretic tradition avoids. Look, for example, at the end of chapter 43 and the beginning of chapter 44. This is clearly a single narrative—one we will discuss in great detail later in this book—and most modern editors would be confounded by the insertion of a new chapter here.

Traditional Hebrew Text[21] unless otherwise indicated. This translation is available in the public domain and with a free public license thanks to Sefaria (www.sefaria.org), a nonprofit organization that, in its own words, is dedicated to assembling "a free, living library of Jewish texts."

---

21. Philadelphia: Jewish Publication Society, 1985.

Introduction for the Curious Student

How many Passover seders have you been to? Six? Seven? More than you can remember? Regardless of the exact number, you probably think you already know the story of the exodus from Egypt pretty well, and you may well be right.

If that's the case, you may be wondering, Why am I about to start reading a book about Exodus?

That's a fair question. Are you ready for an honest answer (or maybe even more than one answer)?

Let's state the obvious. There are some things in life that there is no reason to revisit once you learn them. Basic math facts are a good example. Once you learn that two plus two equals four, you're done. No need to ever relearn that fact.

Other subjects, like science, need to be reviewed all the time because scientists and researchers are always making new discoveries, which means that the facts you once thought you knew may not be correct.

Of course, the Five Books of Moses (or the Pentateuch, as these books are often called) are old texts. People have been studying them literally for thousands of years. (And you thought four or five seders were a lot!) There certainly can't be anything new in books that old.

The reason for going back and studying a book like Exodus for a second or third or fourth time is that it is possible to discover new lessons and insights with each reading. Maybe you already know the story of how Moses's mother put him in a wicker basket in the Nile River after he was born. If so, you know that she did this in an effort to save his life. But do you know the role his sister Miriam played in saving his life? Or how she made his birth even possible?

Perhaps you remember from your many seders that Pharaoh would not let the Jews leave Egypt. Did you ever stop and ask why? The plagues were destroying his country and his people. Why was he being so stubborn? Why not let the people go?

What about the Jewish people standing before God at Mount Sinai and receiving the Ten Commandments? (Spoiler alert . . . keep reading, and you'll discover that there were *not* ten commandments given to the Jews at Mount Sinai.) The only mention of this at the Passover seder is: "If He had brought us before Mount Sinai and had not given us the Torah, Dayenu, it would have been enough!"

By now it should be clear that while you may know some or perhaps many stories from Exodus, there is still much you can learn about and from the book. And that's what *this* book is all about. Helping you learn new lessons from familiar stories that you can apply to your life.

There is one other thing for you to learn from this book, and that is the importance of asking questions. This book is filled with questions, some of which you may have thought of and others that may have never entered your mind. By the end of this book, you will have seen that asking questions is something all of us need to do if we want to really learn what we're studying. And this is true even when there are no good answers to our questions and even when there are *no* answers to our questions.

Ready to learn some new things from an old story you may already know? Let's get started.

Family Tree of Moses

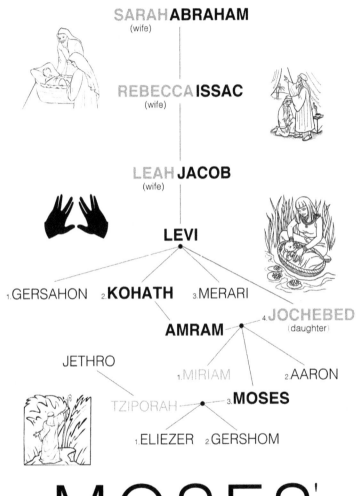

SARAH **ABRAHAM**
(wife)

REBECCA **ISSAC**
(wife)

LEAH **JACOB**
(wife)

LEVI

1.GERSAHON   2.**KOHATH**   3.MERARI

AMRAM   4.JOCHEBED
(daughter)

JETHRO

1.MIRIAM   2.AARON

TZIPORAH   3.**MOSES**

1.ELIEZER   2.GERSHOM

MOSES'
FAMILY TREE

Shemot

(Exod 1:1–6:1)

Part One (for Parents and Educators)—One Book or Two

Regardless of their age, students who study Exodus typically begin their discussions with two basic questions, both of which involve the opening verse of the book: "And these are the names of the sons of Israel who came to Egypt with Jacob, each coming with his household." The text goes on to list the names of Jacob's twelve sons.

The first question is rather obvious. The final chapters of Genesis tell the story of Jacob and his sons and their arrival in Egypt in great detail. Why start Exodus with "old news"? Anyone who reads the five books of the Pentateuch in their correct order already knows the names of "the sons of Israel who came to Egypt"!

The rabbinic tradition as reflected in the midrash has an answer to this question. Even though the Pentateuch (in the book of Genesis) lists Jacob's sons by name in their lifetimes, it lists their names again in Exodus when it tells us of their deaths ("Joseph died, and all his brothers, and all that generation"). The reason is simply to let us know how much Jacob and his sons are loved by God.

This idea that listing names, which is a form of counting, shows God's love for the Jewish people arises again when one studies the book of Numbers. In Numbers, God counts the entire nation not once but twice (which explains why the name of this book in English is "Numbers"). The midrash has a beautiful metaphor to explain these countings. Imagine a travelling salesperson who has a bag of diamonds to sell. Each night, when his day has ended and he is getting ready to go to sleep, he has one last thing to do: count the diamonds. He counts and recounts them because each one is special, and each one is precious. So, too, are the Jewish people in the eyes of God, and that is why He counts and recounts them.

The second question on the opening verse of Exodus requires some thought, especially after we have an explanation for the repetition of the names of Jacob's sons. Take another look at the verse, and you will notice that it starts with the word "and." (If your English translation omits the word "and," as many do, it is not an accurate translation of the Hebrew!) This is strange. "And" serves as a connecting word, but this is the very first verse of Exodus. What is this word connecting the verse to? There can only be one answer: the book of Genesis. In other words, it is possible to understand this word "and" as making a single book out of Genesis and Exodus.

If you stop and think about it, this doesn't seem so crazy. Just look at the overall story both books come to teach us. Genesis tells us of the creation of the world but quickly turns its focus to the origins of the Jewish people. An important part of this origin story, maybe even the most important part, is the story of the Jewish people going down to Egypt and their exodus from there. In other words, Genesis and Exodus are telling us one long story, and so, perhaps they really are one book!

In practical terms, we count Genesis and Exodus as separate books. (Remember, the Pentateuch has five books, not four.) Yet they are deeply connected thematically, and that is what the word "and" comes to teach us.

Shemot

(Exod 1:1–6:1)

Part Two—A New and Difficult Chapter Begins

Summary of This Week's Reading

In this week's reading, Jacob's descendants (who are called "Hebrews" by the Egyptians) face a new and difficult chapter in their story of becoming the Jewish people. We learn that all of Jacob's sons have died, but their children and their children's children "multiplied and increased very greatly, so that the land was filled with them." This concerns the new king (his title, like that of all the rulers of Egypt who came before and after him, was "Pharaoh"), and he decides that he must find a solution to this "Hebrew problem." His solution? Make them slaves and make them work very hard. That way, they will be too tired to have so many children.

It is a good plan in theory, but God has other plans for the emerging Jewish nation, as the Torah tells us: "But the more they [the Hebrews] were oppressed, the more they increased and spread out, so that the [Egyptians] came to dread [fear] the Israelites." Pharaoh then summons the Hebrew midwives (women specially trained to help mothers deliver their babies). He tells them that they must kill all the baby boys they help the Hebrew women deliver. But the midwives (it is unclear whether they are Egyptian or Hebrew) are righteous and fear God. They refuse to obey Pharaoh's order.

As you can imagine, this makes Pharaoh very angry, and he orders his soldiers to throw all newborn baby boys into the Nile. It is at

3

this time that Moses is born. His mother is able to hide him for three months. (Just how she is able to do so is also unclear.) Ultimately, she is forced to put baby Moses in the Nile River in a waterproofed basket. All his mother can do is pray for him, but his big sister Miriam goes to watch over him. She sees Pharaoh's daughter come to the river to bathe, and when Pharaoh's daughter sees the basket and hears the baby crying, she takes pity on him and decides to raise him as her own son. Miriam then steps forward and offers to bring a Hebrew nursemaid for the child. Pharaoh's daughter agrees to the suggestion, and Miriam calls the child's mother to nurse baby Moses.

Moses grows up in Pharaoh's palace. Years pass, and one day, he goes out to see his real people, the Hebrews. What does he see? An Egyptian beating a Hebrew. This makes Moses so angry that he kills the Egyptian. When Pharaoh hears what Moses has done, Moses realizes that he must run away, far away. He goes to a land called Midian. There, he rescues a group of sisters from some wicked shepherds. (The sisters had gathered by a well to water their father Jethro's sheep.) Moses ends up marrying the oldest of the sisters, Zipporah. She becomes pregnant and gives birth to a son, Gershom.

Back in Egypt, life for the Hebrew slaves becomes worse and worse. They cry out to God, and He remembers the promises He made to their forefathers, Abraham, Isaac, and Jacob. And so, God puts His plan to save the Jewish people in motion.

Step one is to find a leader who can take the people out of Egypt. This, as we all know, is Moses. But how to break this news to Moses? God does so by appearing to Moses in a burning bush. Moses sees this bush and sees that the fire has no effect on it! This is amazing, thinks Moses, and he decides to head toward the bush for a closer look. Once Moses is standing next to the burning bush, God calls out to him and tells him that He has decided that it is time to free the Jews from their Egyptian masters.

God goes on to give Moses specific instructions: He is to gather the Israelite elders and tell them that God has remembered them and will now rescue them from Egypt and bring them to a land of milk and honey. Next, Moses must go to Pharaoh and ask permission to leave along with the Israelites. But, God tells Moses, Pharaoh will not listen and will not let the people go. *In the end, though, this will not matter, God says, because He will "smite Egypt with a strong arm," which will convince Pharaoh to free the Hebrews.*

So that Pharaoh will know that Moses has been sent by God, God gives Moses three miracles to show to the people. But Moses still does not believe that he is up to the task, because he stutters. God therefore assigns his brother Aaron to be Moses's spokesperson.

Moses quickly packs up his things and heads to Egypt with his wife and sons. (A second son, Eliezer, was born to Moses just before he left.) On the way, Moses meets Aaron, who has come from Egypt to greet him, and together they go to Egypt, gather the elders, and perform the wondrous signs that God gave Moses.

Soon afterward, Moses and Aaron go to Pharaoh, who laughs at their request that he free the Hebrews. Not only does he deny their request, he gives the Hebrew slaves much more work to do! The new work is too much for them, and when the Hebrews fail to complete their new tasks, they are beaten by their Egyptian taskmasters.

All this saddens and confuses Moses. He turns to God and asks: "O Lord, why did You bring harm upon this people? Why did You send me? Ever since I came to Pharaoh to speak in Your name, he has dealt worse with this people; and still You have not delivered Your people."

God is not pleased with the doubts Moses expresses, but He reassures Moses by telling him that he will soon see what God has planned for Pharaoh. Pharaoh may say "no" now, but he will *let the people go.*

Life Lessons from *Shemot*

The first weekly reading in Exodus covers a lot of ground, from the start of the Jews becoming slaves in Egypt, to the birth and rescue of baby Moses, to God choosing Moses for the important mission of leading the Jews out of Egypt, to Moses's first meeting with Pharaoh. That's a lot of material to choose from as we begin to think about some of the life lessons we can learn from this book of the Pentateuch.

With this in mind, let's look at three stories that have much to teach us.

Who Says You're Too Little

As we have already seen, Jacob's children and grandchildren are living in Egypt when the book of Exodus begins. Since Egypt is in Africa, it seems appropriate to begin our first life lesson with an African proverb: "If you think you are too small to make a difference, you haven't spent a night with a mosquito."

Perhaps you're wondering, What do mosquitos have to do with the Exodus story? Good question. (Although, as we will see, the third plague God brings down upon Egypt involves lice, and lice are small, annoying insects like mosquitos—but that's a bit of a stretch, don't you think?)

The connection between this week's reading and mosquitos can be summed up in one word: Miriam. Here's how: Miriam is six years old when Moses is born. (She is also three years older than Aaron.) Very often, adults will tell six-year-old children that they are too little to do this or that. But Miriam does not seem to think of herself as too little to do anything. Want proof? Here are two amazing things that she accomplishes in this week's reading even though she is only six.

We know that Pharaoh is very afraid of the Jews living in Egypt—so afraid that he makes them slaves and then orders his soldiers to kill all the baby boys born to Jewish mothers. The text gives us few details beyond this, so the midrash fills the gaps in the story.

According to the midrash, Miriam's father, Amram, is the leader of the Jewish people in Egypt, and when he hears about the order to kill baby boys, he separates himself from his wife so that they will not risk having a baby boy. Soon, all the Jewish men in Egypt follow Amram's example and separate themselves from their wives. What does little Miriam do? She says to Amram, "'Father, your decree is worse than Pharaoh's; Pharaoh decrees only against the males, whereas you decree against the males and females."[1]

How was Amram's decree worse than that of Pharaoh? Miriam reminds her father that Pharaoh's terrible order applies only to baby boys. Baby girls will be allowed to live. But if husbands and wives stay apart, there will be no baby boys *or* baby girls. That's a very clever argument for a six-year-old to make, and once Amram hears his daughter, he knows she is right. He immediately returns to his wife, Jochebed, and the other Jewish men go back to their wives, too.

Were it not for Miriam's timely advice, Moses would never have been born! What's more, after Moses is born, her actions save his life. How does Miriam accomplish this second amazing feat?

Moses is born early. The text does not tell us exactly how premature he is, but somehow his mother Jochebed is able to hide him from Pharaoh's soldiers (who are always searching for newborn baby boys) for three months. By this time, Moses is too big to hide, so Jochebed puts him in a wicker basket and then places the basket among the reeds growing along the banks of the Nile River. She hopes that perhaps some Egyptian woman will find her baby, take pity on him, and take him home to raise as her own son. But how can Jochebed be sure that someone will save baby Moses? Again, we can answer this question with one word: Miriam.

Brave little Miriam hides along the riverbank to keep an eye on her baby brother. And who should come down to the river just at that moment? Pharaoh's daughter! She hears the baby crying and tells her slave girl to bring her the basket. When she sees baby Moses, she takes pity on him. At this moment, Miriam bursts out from her hiding place and says to Pharaoh's daughter, the princess of Egypt, "Shall I go and get you a Hebrew woman to nurse the child for you?"

Think about this for just one minute. Miriam is a Hebrew, and the Hebrews are slaves. How dare any slave, especially a child, speak to Pharaoh's daughter? And how dare this child

---

1. This midrash is, of course, not found in the text of this week's reading. It is instead told in the Talmud (Sotah 12a).

tell Pharaoh's daughter what to do? But like Amram, Pharaoh's daughter sees that Miriam is offering very good advice, so she listens to this six-year-old child. And who is the Hebrew woman Miriam brings to Pharaoh's daughter to nurse baby Moses? His real mother, Jochebed! Jochebed nurses baby Moses for many, many months—possibly even for years.[2] During this time, she makes sure that Moses knows who is people really are. In this way, Miriam not only helps save his life, but she helps make sure Moses grows up knowing that he is really Jewish.

Now it should be clear what that African proverb has to do with our story. Miriam may have been small—maybe as small as a mosquito to some adults—but she certainly made a difference in the lives and the history of the Jewish people.

> Can you think of a time when someone told you that you were too little to do something? Why was that? Can you think of a time you did something anyway, even after being told you were too little? What made you think you could do it?

Forgetting the Past is Never a Good Idea

"How" is a very curious word. Sometimes when you use it to ask a question, you are looking for an explanation of a process. For example, when we ask, How did the Jews become slaves to Pharaoh in Egypt?, what we really what to know is, What did Pharaoh do to make the Jews slaves? Did he trick them somehow? Did he force them into slavery?

This week's reading gives us a pretty simple answer to this question. Pharaoh feels threatened by the ever-increasing number of Jews in his country. He even thinks that they may join Egypt's enemies if war ever breaks out. His solution to this potential threat is to make the Jews his slaves.

But this answer is not as simple as it seems. The text says that Pharaoh had a "shrewd" (clever or sneaky) plan to enslave the

---

2. In those days, it was not uncommon for babies to nurse until the age of three.

Jews. However, the text then goes on to say, "They set taskmasters over them to oppress them with forced labor; and they built garrison cities for Pharaoh: Pithom and Raamses." Something seems to be missing. Pharaoh's shrewd plan is to force the Jews to be slaves? That doesn't seem so shrewd, but a remarkable midrash gives us more details about Pharaoh's plan.

It seems that when Pharaoh decides to enslave the Jews, he declares a national week of labor. All good citizens are asked to come and help in the building of the cities of Pithom and Raamses, with Pharaoh himself in the lead. The Jews, of course, want to show that they, too, are good and loyal citizens, and they quickly join in. Imagine their surprise when they show up for work on day two and find that there are no Egyptians there to work! There are only Jews, and these Jews quickly find themselves surrounded by taskmasters who demand that they do the same amount of work they did voluntarily the day before. Now, that's shrewd!

Let's return to the word "how." There is another way to think about the question, How did the Jews become slaves? Maybe what we are really asking is, How could this happen? What about all the good Joseph, a Jew, did for Egypt? He saved the country from famine! How could Pharaoh turn around and make Joseph's descendants slaves?

Once again, this week's reading gives us a simple answer: "A new king arose over Egypt who did not know Joseph." This seems crazy. How could he not know Joseph? That's like an American student not knowing who George Washington or Abraham Lincoln was! What's going on here?

Of course, Pharaoh knows who Joseph is. He is just acting as if he didn't. Pharaoh doesn't want to be bound by the past, so he decides to forget it (or ignore it). If he "forgets" all the good Joseph did for Egypt, there's no reason he can't make slaves out of Joseph's descendants.

What can we learn from this?

Our history—who we are as individuals, as families, as a people—is important. If shapes us. It guides us. Sometimes it helps us avoid making bad decisions (especially if someone in our past made the same decision and we know how badly things turned out). In other words, history is too important to be ignored or forgotten.

Pharaoh's big mistake is that he values the present more than the past. He wants what he wants (that is, to make the Jews into slaves), so history doesn't matter to him. This leads him to make a series of bad decisions, like enslaving the Jews, ignoring the plagues God brings down on Egypt, and refusing to let the Jews go. And in the end, Pharaoh and all his people suffer the consequences of his ignoring history.

This certainly is a lesson worth not forgetting!

> *Do your parents ever share stories with you from when they were little? Do they talk about mistakes they made when sharing these stories? Can you remember one story in particular that helped you avoid making a bad decision?*

The Importance of Seeing the Wonders of Life

As we saw in the summary of this week's reading, the first step in God's plan to free the Jews from slavery is to find the right leader. We all know that leader is Moses. The question is, How and why did God pick him?

Good leaders, especially those taking on a job as difficult as leading the Jews out of slavery, need certain character traits to succeed. A leader must be humble to understand what his or her true contributions are. Good leaders are important, but they cannot do things on their own. Humble leaders understand this, and Moses is described in the Torah as the most humble of all people. However, this is not why God chooses Moses.

Good leaders need to be sensitive to the needs of their followers, and there is a story about the time Moses tended the flocks of Jethro that illustrates how sensitive Moses was.

The midrash tells us that Moses always watched over the flocks with loving care. He would lead the young animals to pasture first so that they would have the most tender, juicy grass for their food. Next, he would bring the slightly older animals out, and these he allowed to eat the herbs best suited to them. Only after both groups had eaten did Moses bring out the strongest and largest members of the flock. These he let eat the hard grass that was left, because it was good for them and because the weaker animals couldn't eat it. When God saw this, He said, "He who understands how to pasture sheep and to provide for each what is good for it is the one who should pasture My people."

Nice, but there's more. It's also important for good leaders to be compassionate, and Moses was very compassionate and very caring, as illustrated by another story from the midrash.

One day, a baby goat escaped from the flocks. Moses followed it, and what did he see? He saw how the baby goat stopped at each stream or water hole it came to. Moses drew close to the baby goat and said, "Poor animal, I did not know that you were so thirsty and that you ran away only to look for water to drink." Moses then noticed how tired the little animal was, and so, he gently picked it up, put it on his shoulder, and carried it back to the herd. When God saw this, He said, "You have compassion with a flock belonging to a man of flesh and blood! As you live, you shall pasture Israel, My flock."

This is a beautiful story, and it shows that Moses's great compassion helped God decide to make him the leader of the Jewish people. But there is an even better reason for Moses being picked, and we see it in this week's reading.

Remember the burning bush? It burned for quite some time. Many people passed it, but none turned aside to take a closer look, except for Moses. He saw the bush burn, and he saw that the burning fire had no effect on the bush. Moses understood that he was seeing something wondrous and miraculous. Of course, he had to take a closer look, and when he did, God spoke to him. Only then did God say to Moses, "Come, therefore, I will send you to Pharaoh, and you shall free My people, the Israelites, from Egypt."

Were Moses not humble, caring, and compassionate, God never would have selected him to lead the Jewish people. These were character traits that the person who would lead the Jews out of Egypt had to have. But the person God had in mind for this mission needed something else as well. He needed the ability to see and appreciate the wonders and miracles of life. It was this final trait that made Moses the right person for the job.

We can learn a lot from this story. There are so many wonders all around us to see if only we stop and take the time to look for them. And when we do, we gain a better appreciation for God and all that God does for humankind.

Think about it this way: it's hard to be thankful to God if we don't notice all that God gives us.

> *Not all of life's wonders involve miracles. A baby being born or the flowers blooming again in the spring are truly wondrous, but such things are part of our normal, day-to-day lives. What event or thing in your daily life do you think is most wondrous? Have you always thought of it as wondrous, or did you learn over time to think of it that way?*

Va'era

(Exod 6:2–9:35)

Part One (for Parents and Educators)—Why Does God Harden Pharaoh's Heart?

This week's reading forces us to think about one of the hardest questions that comes up in the book of Exodus. But to understand the question, we must first discuss a very important and very difficult concept in Judaism. You may not have even heard about it, and you may not completely get it, even after reading this chapter. That's okay, because there are many adults who don't fully get it either.

Are you ready to give it a shot? Good. Then let's get started.

All people who believe in the one, true God—whether they are Jewish, Christian, or Muslim—believe in a fair and merciful God. One who only wants good for His creations. One who rewards people who do good and punishes people who do evil. No one really understands how and when God rewards people or how and when He punishes people. We just trust God to do this fairly.

There is something important to consider when thinking about reward and punishment, and maybe you have never thought about it in this way. To be rewarded for doing something good (or punished for doing something evil), a person has to have a say in the matter. In other words, if God were to make a person do something—be it good or evil—how would it be fair for God to reward or punish that person? After all, he or she had no choice in the matter. They were "forced" to do it by God.

We call this ability to choose between good and evil without interference "free will." God gives each of us free will, which means that it is up to each person to decide whether to follow God's commandments.

Let's pause for a minute. A commandment is like an order. If God "orders" us to do something, does that mean that we definitely will? The answer is no. God lets us choose whether or not to follow His commandments. In the Torah, He often tells us what the consequences of our choices and our actions will be. There are always consequences, good or bad, that result from our actions. But at the end of the day, we decide, and only after we decide can God judge us and give out rewards and punishments.

Free will is one of the basic principles that define Judaism. Without it, the whole idea that God treats us fairly and rewards or punishes as appropriate makes no sense. This is what makes our reading this week so confusing. We read that God hardens Pharaoh's heart so that he will not let the Jewish slaves leave Egypt, and because Pharaoh does not free the slaves, God punishes him and his people with ten plagues.

What? We just said that God gives people free will to choose to do good or evil. God has to give people free will for their rewards or punishments to make sense and to be fair! So, how can God harden Pharaoh's heart and take away his free will?

This is a very big and very serious question. Of all the answers given to this question, perhaps the best one was suggested by the great Rabbi Moshe ben Nachman, who lived in Girona, Spain, in the early 1200s. To understand his answer, we have to look very carefully at the text of the Exodus story.

When Moses and Aaron first meet with Pharaoh, what is the first thing they say? "Thus says the LORD, the God of Israel: Let My people go that they may celebrate a festival for Me in the wilderness." Pharaoh isn't very impressed with Moses and Aaron or with their God: "Who is the LORD that I should heed Him and let Israel go? I do not know the LORD, nor will I let Israel go." We see clearly that Pharaoh can and does decide to ignore God. Pharaoh's first and real choice is *not* to let the Jews leave Egypt.

What happens next? Plagues—ten plagues to be exact, each worse than the previous one. At first, Pharaoh sticks with his initial decision not to let the Jews go. After all, that is what he really wants. And in fact, if you read the verses very, very carefully, you will see that with each of the first five plagues, Pharaoh hardens his own heart! (To "harden one's heart" is a poetic way of saying that a person is stubborn and refuses to change his or her mind.) God only begins to harden Pharaoh's heart with the sixth plague.

According to Rabbi Moshe, God wants Pharaoh to be able to make his own decision and to stick to that decision. But there's a problem. The plagues were bad. They were scary. They were destroying Egypt. The plagues were about to force Pharaoh to change his mind and let the Jews go *even though he didn't want to!* But if Pharaoh decided to let the Jews go only because the plagues were scary, the decision to let the Jews go would not actually be his, and this, of course, would mean that he had no free will.

This is why, says Rabbi Moshe, God hardens Pharaoh's heart and makes him stubborn. By making Pharaoh so stubborn he can ignore the plagues, God is not taking away his free will. God is protecting Pharaoh's free will. Pharaoh's first and true answer to Moses was, "No! I will not let the people go!" Only because God hardens his heart can Pharaoh show his free will and continue to say no.

Va'era

(Exod 6:2–9:35)

Part Two—The Plagues Arrive

Summary of This Week's Reading

Last week's reading concludes with Moses complaining to God about his first meeting with Pharaoh. The meeting did not go well at all, and Pharaoh ends up giving the Hebrew slaves even more work to do.

God isn't very happy with these complaints. He scolds Moses and tells him that He, God, will surely free the Jewish people from Egypt. In fact, God promises that He will free (or redeem) them in four ways: (1) He will take the Jewish people out from Egypt; (2) He will deliver them from being slaves; (3) He will redeem them and make them His own chosen people at Mount Sinai; and (4) He will then bring them to the land of Israel, which He promised to the patriarchs, Abraham, Isaac, and Jacob.

With this reassurance from God, Moses goes back to meet with Pharaoh (with Aaron as his spokesperson). They stand before Pharaoh and demand that he let the Hebrew slaves go. To show Pharaoh that they really mean business this time, Aaron takes Moses's staff and throws it to the ground. It miraculously turns into a serpent. Pharaoh doesn't think this is a big deal, and he orders his magicians to do the same with their staffs. They do, and so, Pharaoh remains unimpressed and unmoved. He will not let the people go. And thus the plagues begin.

With the first plague there begins a pattern that continues until the end of this week's reading. Moses and Aaron repeatedly come before Pharaoh to demand in the name of God, "Let My people go, so that they may serve Me in the wilderness." Pharaoh repeatedly refuses, and a plague then strikes Egypt.

According to rabbinic tradition, each plague lasts for seven days. (We will talk more about the number seven in the next chapter.) While each plague is going on, Pharaoh seems willing to change his mind, but once it ends, he refuses over and over to free the Jewish people.

We know that in total there are ten plagues. Here are the ones that appear in this week's reading, with some additional details about them from the midrash:

1. **The waters of the Nile River turn to blood.** And not just the Nile but all the waters in Egypt, leaving the people with nothing to drink. Only in Goshen, the part of Egypt where the Jews live, is there water to drink.

2. **Swarms of frogs overrun the land.** And not just the land but every corner of every house. The Egyptians find frogs in their beds. Frogs in their containers of food. Even frogs in their ovens. (Just think how annoying that must have been!) But, of course, there are no frogs in Goshen.

3. **Lice infest the Egyptians and their farm animals.** Lice make people itch, and these lice aren't just in the Egyptians' hair (where lice are usually found) but all over their entire bodies.

4. **Hordes of wild animals invade the cities of Egypt.** They stampede through the streets and through the fields, causing tremendous damage everywhere they go.

5. **A deadly disease kills the Egyptians' farm animals.** Dead cattle mean no milk to drink or meat to eat. Dead sheep mean no wool to use to make clothes. This is a very costly plague. Of course, no animals die in Goshen.

6. **Painful boils strike the Egyptians.** *Boils are disgusting, pus-filled lumps, and they appear on the faces, necks, armpits, shoulders, and buttocks of the Egyptians but not on the Jews.*

7. **Fire and ice combine to create a destructive hailstorm.** *Anyone who ignores Moses's warning and stays outside is badly hurt. Farm animals left outside in the fields are badly hurt, and crops growing in the fields are badly damaged or completely destroyed.*

Despite the pain and suffering these plagues cause the Egyptian people, Pharaoh still refuses to let the Jewish people go, just as God told Moses would happen.

Life Lessons from *Va'era*

Pharaoh emerges as a main character in this week's reading. He is a wicked king who makes the lives of the Hebrew slaves worse and worse and who ends up throwing their babies in the Nile River. You should be asking, what life lessons could we possibly learn from him? That's a fair question, and what we can learn from his actions is how *not* to act.

But before we discuss things we shouldn't do, let's start with Moses and a lesson about something all of us can and should do daily.

The Importance of Showing Gratitude

When Moses first meets God at the burning bush, he argues that he is not the right person to bring the Jews out of Egypt. "I stutter and do not speak well," Moses explains, "and the people will not believe me." God is not convinced by these arguments. "Aaron will be your spokesperson," God replies. And then He continues, "What is in your hand, Moses?"

We all know the answer to this question: Moses has a shepherd's staff in his hand. We aren't sure exactly what it looked like. It was probably little more than a long, wooden stick, but God makes this simple staff a symbol of Moses's power and a sign that God Himself sent Moses back to Egypt to free to Jews from slavery.

So, if you were asked who uses this staff to bring about the first plague (turning all the water in Egypt into blood), you would surely say, Moses. What about the second plague (frogs) and the third plague (lice)? Moses, right? Wrong. It is Aaron who takes Moses's staff and strikes the Nile River, turning it to blood. It is Aaron who holds the staff over the Nile to bring swarms of frogs from the river to cover the land of Egypt. And it is Aaron who again takes the staff and strikes the dust of Egypt, turning it into lice, which quickly infest every person, including Pharaoh's magicians. (We will talk more about the magicians shortly.)

What's going on here? Why isn't Moses using his own staff to bring about these plagues? The answer to this question is very simple: Moses is showing gratitude to the river and to the dust of the earth.

This is not as strange as it first appears. Remember that when Moses's mother could no longer hide him from the Egyptian soldiers who were looking to throw newborn Jewish babies into the Nile, she put him in a wicker basket and set him afloat in the waters of the Nile. And it is from the Nile that Pharaoh's daughter saved baby Moses. So in a way, the water saved Moses's life, and in a show of gratitude, Moses does not strike the river to turn it to blood or to bring countless frogs from it. He lets Aaron do this.

Moses also owes a debt of gratitude to the dust of Egypt. If you recall, when Moses first left Pharaoh's palace to see what life was like for his Jewish brothers and sisters, he saw an Egyptian taskmaster brutally beating a Jewish slave. Moses grew furious at this sight and killed the Egyptian to save the Jew. This may be a brave act, but it is a dangerous one for an Egyptian prince like Moses. To kill another Egyptian to save a Jew? Unheard of!

Recognizing the danger, Moses moved quickly to hide the body of the dead Egyptian. But where? In the sand and dust along the Nile River—the very same sand and dust that Aaron strikes with the staff to turn it into lice. Once again, Moses lets Aaron perform the miracle, and in doing so, Moses shows gratitude to the sand and dust.

Wow. If Moses shows gratitude to non-living things like a river and the sand alongside the river, how much more should we show gratitude to the living people who do good things for us? That's a lesson worth remembering and acting upon every day!

> What was the last important thing someone did for you that made you stop and say, "thank you"? Did you thank that person right away? Did you do anything else to show him or her how grateful you were? Do you think that saying "thank you" made it more likely that this person would do something for you again?

The Dangers of Being Stubborn

By now, we know that Pharaoh's first and true reaction to Moses's request that he free the Hebrew slaves is to say no. ("I do not know the LORD, nor will I let Israel go.") Pharaoh isn't very impressed with the God of the Hebrews or with His messenger Moses. And, truth be told, neither are his magicians, and the text tells us why.

In an effort to prove to Pharaoh His seriousness about letting the Jews go, God gives Moses the power to turn his shepherd's staff into a snake. The problem is, Pharaoh's magicians can also turn staffs into snakes![1] These magicians can (according to the midrash) also turn water into blood, and they do so after Aaron uses Moses's staff to turn the water of Egypt into blood. (Where they get water to turn into blood is a big question.) Frogs? Just like Aaron, the magicians bring frogs up out of the Nile. Only when the lice come are the magicians unable to copy what Aaron does. In fact, they are covered with lice themselves, just like everyone else in Egypt.

At this point, the magicians see the truth for what it is. They can perform certain tricks and copy some things Aaron does with the staff, but they at last understand the power of God. They frantically say to Pharaoh as they plead with him to listen to Moses, "This is the finger of God!" After the plague of hail, the other advisors to Pharaoh speak more harshly and more honestly than the magicians. They say to Pharaoh, "Do you not see what is going on here? Egypt is being destroyed because you will not let the Hebrew slaves go!"

Stubborn Pharaoh! He cannot and will not see the truth. He would rather be stubborn than admit the reality of the situation. It is as if he were saying to his magicians and his other advisors,

---

1. The magicians could certainly copy this miraculous action, but they should have realized the limits of their power. The text (Exod 7:11–12) tells us why and exactly what happens: "Then Pharaoh, for his part, summoned the wise men and the sorcerers; and the Egyptian magicians, in turn, did the same with their spells; each cast down his rod, and they turned into serpents. But Aaron's rod swallowed their rods." In other words, Aaron's snake/staff turned back into a staff and only then ate the snakes the Egyptian magicians had conjured up!

"I am right. Only I know what is best for Egypt. Only I know the correct thing to do." But, sadly for the Egyptians, he doesn't.

More Dangers of Being Stubborn

It is a terrible thing to be so stubborn that you cannot see the truth for what it is. But Pharaoh's stubbornness involves more than just ignoring the facts around him. Because of his stubbornness, people suffer. Just go through the list of the plagues (seven in all) that are described in this week's reading to see how much the Egyptian people suffered because of Pharaoh's stubbornness.

As we have already mentioned, the rabbinic tradition is that each plague lasted for seven days, and so, for seven days, the Egyptians had no water to drink, because the Nile turned to blood. For seven days, there were frogs in every corner of their homes, from their beds to their ovens. For seven days, the people itched and scratched because of the lice that covered them. For seven days, wild animals stampeded through the streets of their towns and villages. For seven days, the people watched helplessly as their cattle died. For seven days, they were covered with boils. For seven days, fiery hail fell and destroyed almost all their crops.

Is it any wonder that Pharaoh's aides beg him to look at the peoples' suffering and to feel their pain? But he can't. All he can see and feel is his own stubbornness.

And so, the important life lesson we learn from Pharaoh's story is how dangerous and selfish it is to be stubborn and to insist that only you know the right thing to do. Pharaoh is convinced that he knows what to do better than anyone else. He is wrong, and his people pay the price for his stubbornness.

> *Think of a time when you were stubborn. Did that prove to be a good thing? Can you truthfully say that something good ever came out of you being stubborn?*

Bo

(Exod 10:1–13:16)

Part One (for Parents and Educators)—Why These Particular Plagues?

In last week's reading, we asked a very important and very hard question: why did God harden Pharaoh's heart? This week's reading leads us to two more difficult questions.

First, why did God send ten plagues? Wouldn't one have been enough, especially if it was the last one, found in this week's reading, where God kills the Egyptians' firstborn?

Second (and this question is related to the first), why these ten plagues? God could have used any terrible thing to make the Egyptians free their Hebrew slaves. Why blood, frogs, lice, and so on?

Let's start with some numbers that often appear in our biblical stories. Each is important in its own way and for its own reasons. For instance, the number three. Three represents the idea of completeness, because it symbolizes having a beginning, middle, and end. In the Torah, the number three also has special religious significance. For example, there are three patriarchs (Abraham, Isaac, and Jacob) and three groupings of the Jewish people (*Kohen*, those descended from Aaron in his role of High Priest; *Levi*, those whose ancestors assisted the priests in the temple; and *Yisrael*, everyone else).

Four is another special number, and not only because there are four matriarchs (Sarah, Rebekah, Rachel, and Leah) but also because there are four rivers that flow from the Garden of Eden. In the construction of the special furniture used in the tabernacle (called *mishkan* in Hebrew) that Moses builds in the desert so the people can worship God, we find the number four again and again in the measurements of its furniture. And, of course, we see the number four throughout the Exodus story and the yearly seder held to remember this event: four cups of wine, four questions, and four sons.

In the Bible, the number seven is also central to many stories: the seven days of creation, Noah bringing seven clean beasts into the ark, the Jews traveling for seven weeks after they leave Egypt to arrive at Mount Sinai, and God telling Moses to build a special candelabra with seven branches (called a *menorah* in Hebrew) to be used in the tabernacle (and later in the temple). Seven is also an important part of Jewish religious observance: the major festivals of Passover and Sukkot are both seven days long,[1] we celebrate marriages for seven days, and we mourn for the deceased for seven days. And the list of sevens goes on and on.

Finally, we arrive at the number ten. We find in the Torah a series of tens, also starting with creation. If you look closely at the creation story found in the first chapters of Genesis, you will find that God creates the heavens and the earth with ten utterances, or statements.[2] There are ten generations from Adam to Noah and ten generations from Noah to Abraham. A more famous example of the number ten is the "Ten Commandments." (In an upcoming chapter, we will ask whether they are really "commandments" or just "utterances.")

---

1. The biblical command is to observe both holidays for seven days, and this is the practice in the land of Israel. However, Jews living outside the land of Israel observe these holidays for eight days.

2. If you counted carefully, you only found the phrase "And God said" nine times! The sages of the Talmud saw this, too, but here is how they arrived at the number ten: "With ten utterances the world was created. And what is learned: 'And He said' is written nine times, from 'In the beginning' (Gen 1:1) to 'And completed' (Gen 2:1). And 'In the beginning' is also an utterance, as it is stated (Ps 33:6), 'By the word of the Lord the heavens were made'—as it is impossible that the heavens and the earth were created without an utterance" (Rabbeinu Yonah in his commentary to Avot 5:1).

And this, of course, brings us to the ten plagues and to our question, Why ten plagues? The rabbis of the Talmud ask this very same question about the ten utterances God used to create the world, and their answer can also answer our question about the plagues. They say that the world was created with ten utterances (rather than with just one) in order to punish people who sin and do bad things and to reward those who do what is right.

What exactly does this mean? Here is the simple explanation.

God could have created the world with one utterance, but He took his time and used ten. By taking his time, God is showing us how special the world is, which means that people who do bad things—who in a sense try to destroy or damage God's special world—deserve to be punished. So, too, people who do good and thus build up and protect God's special world deserve a reward.

We can apply this same logic to the Egyptians. The Hebrew slaves, the descendants of Abraham, Isaac, and Jacob, are very special to God. He therefore brings down ten terrible plagues to punish the Egyptians and to show them how special the Hebrews are to Him. Yes, the Egyptians could have been punished with one plague, but they would have missed the lesson about God's special connection with the Jewish people.

This still leaves us with our question of why God chose these particular plagues. There are a number of fascinating answers to this question. One says that these plagues were chosen by God to punish the Egyptians measure for measure for their harsh treatment of the Jews. The table below illustrates this idea of measure for measure:

What the Egyptians Did to the Jews	What God Did to the Egyptians
They made the Jews drawers of water . . .	so their river was turned to **blood**.
They made the Jews load their food and belongings . . .	so the **frogs** destroyed it.
They made the Jews sweep the streets . . .	so the dust turned into **lice**.

What the Egyptians Did to the Jews	What God Did to the Egyptians
They made the Jews babysit their children . . .	so God overran the country with **wild animals** that devoured the children.
They made the Jews cattle-herders . . .	so the **pestilence** killed the herds.
They used the Jews to prepare their baths . . .	so they developed **boils**, which made it impossible for them to wash.
The Jews were made into stone-cutters . . .	And God sent **hailstones** against the Egyptians.
The Jews were forced to tend the vineyards and fields . . .	so the **locusts** consumed all that grew.
The Egyptians sought to keep the Jews as prisoners . . .	so they were themselves made prisoners by the thick **darkness** that fell upon Egypt.
They drowned Jews babies in the Nile . . .	which brought about the **killing of the firstborn**, not to mention their deaths by drowning in the Sea of Reeds.[3]

There is one last factor that can help us understand why God chose these specific plagues, and it has to do with the purpose of the plagues. Yes, it is true that the plagues were meant to punish the Egyptians for their cruel treatment of their Hebrew slaves. But there is more to it than that.

If you recall, when Moses first meets with Pharaoh and asks that he let the Hebrews go to worship God in the wilderness, Pharaoh says: "Who is the LORD that I should heed Him and let Israel go? I do not know the LORD, nor will I let Israel go." God understands from this answer that He not only has to punish Pharaoh and the people of Egypt but also has to teach them that there is a God.

3. In the Exodus story, the body of water that God splits and in which the Egyptian army drowns is called *Yam Suf*. While this Hebrew phrase is typically translated as "the Red Sea," that translation is incorrect. The phrase is correctly translated as "the Sea of Reeds," and the exact location of this body of water is much debated.

Pharaoh denies God on three levels. First, Pharaoh claims that there is no God. After the first three plagues, he admits his mistake, but he still claims that the God of the Hebrews is no more powerful than the Egyptian gods. Three plagues later, Pharaoh changes his mind and agrees that the God of the Hebrews is more powerful than his gods. But he is not convinced that God is all-powerful and that He governs the whole world. It seems like the plagues of fiery hail, huge swarms of locusts, and three days of darkness proved to Pharaoh that God does, in fact, control everything.

In the end, there is a common element to all these answers as to why God chose these particular plagues. As the plagues came, one after the other, they demonstrated to all the people of Egypt the impossibility of fighting God.

Bo

(Exod 10:1–13:16)

Part Two—Freedom Knocks

Summary of This Week's Reading

This week's reading tells us about the last three of the ten plagues. The first of these is the plague of locusts. Moses warns Pharaoh that locusts will strike Egypt in a swarm that is unlike any in the country's history. Pharaoh's advisors beg him to listen to Moses and let the Hebrew slaves go free. They argue that Egypt is being destroyed because of Pharaoh's stubbornness. But Pharaoh will not listen to them or change his mind. And so, the locusts come and destroy any crops that somehow survived the plague of hail.

Next comes the plague of darkness, which is not like any darkness the Egyptians have ever experienced. It is a darkness that can be touched! It lasts for three days, and according to the midrash, the Egyptians can't even get up from where they are. Of course, as with the other plagues, this darkness does not affect the Jews living in Goshen.

The darkness seems to have an impact on Pharaoh. He tells Moses that the people may leave Egypt to worship their God in the desert but only if they leave their cattle behind. Moses rejects this condition, and so Pharaoh sends him away, warning him never to appear in his presence again, "for on the day that you see my face, you shall die!" Moses agrees, but not before he delivers a final message from God about the last and most terrible plague: at around midnight on the fifteenth day of the Hebrew month of Nissan, God will strike dead all the firstborn of Egypt!

God now gives a second message to Moses, but one that is for the Jews only. Moses tells the people that they are to ask the Egyptians for jewels, silver, and gold. Why? Because when God tells Abraham that his descendants will someday be slaves, God promises Abraham that his descendants will go out of slavery with great wealth. The people do as Moses commands, and the Egyptians hand over their valuables to the Jews.

At this point in the story, we read about the first commandments God gives to the Jewish people. The very first of these is to create a calendar based on the monthly cycle of the moon. (The Jewish people need this in order to know when to celebrate holidays like Passover and the New Year.) God also instructs the Jews to bring a "Passover offering": a lamb or kid goat that is to be slaughtered and its blood sprinkled on the doorposts of every Jewish home. This is so that God can pass over these homes when He comes to kill the Egyptian firstborn. (And now you know why the holiday is called "Passover.") But the blood is not the only part of the Passover offering the Jews are to use. They are also to eat the roasted meat of the offering, together with matzah (unleavened bread) and bitter herbs, on the night the firstborn of Egypt are killed.

After telling us about these commandments, the story returns to the plagues. The death of the firstborn is too much for Pharaoh. He finally understands that he must free the Hebrew slaves. But after saying no for so long, Pharaoh cannot wait to get them out of his land. He makes them leave so quickly that there is no time for their dough to rise, and thus the only bread they take with them is unleavened bread.

The reading concludes with one more commandment: the Jews are to observe the anniversary of the Exodus from Egypt each year by removing all leaven (things like bread, crackers, and cookies) from their homes for seven days. And during those seven days they are only to eat matzah with their meals. Most important of all, they are to remember the story of the Exodus by telling it to their children each year (which is why there are Passover seders) and by wearing tefillin on their arms and heads during their daily morning prayer services. (The illustration here shows what tefillin look like.)

Life Lessons from *Bo*

The focus of this week's and last week's readings has been the ten plagues, which is understandable, given how miraculous they are. However, there is a lot going on in this week's reading other than the plagues, and these parts also contain some very good life lessons. Ready to see what they are?

Using Your Time Wisely

Most people are familiar with the story of Mount Sinai, where God appears to the newly freed Hebrew slaves and gives them a set of laws often called the "Ten Commandments." (God actually gives them many more commandments than these ten, but that is a topic we will return to later in this book.) Most people think that these are the first commandments God gives the Jewish people. But most people are wrong, because God gives them a series of commandments while they are still slaves in Egypt.

If you had to guess (and had not just read the summary of this week's reading), what would you think the very first commandment God gave to the Jewish people was? Keep the Sabbath?

Observe dietary laws? Maybe something more basic, like believe in and worship only one God? These would be good but incorrect guesses. As we saw above, the first commandment given to the Jewish people involves their calendar.

A calendar? Really? And one based on the moon? Let's spend a little time on how this calendar works, and then we can talk about the whys of a calendar based on the moon and not the sun.

Here's how a calendar based on the moon works: Toward the beginning of the moon's cycle, it appears as a thin curve (sometimes called a "crescent"). This crescent tells us that it is time to start a new month. Then the moon grows until it is full (we all know what a full moon looks like). This happens in the middle of the month. From this point, the moon grows smaller and smaller until it cannot be seen. It remains invisible for approximately two days, and then the thin crescent appears again, and the cycle starts over.

The phases of the moon: from full to new and back to full

The entire cycle takes approximately twenty-nine and a half days. Since a month needs to have a complete number of days, a Jewish month sometimes has twenty-nine days (such a month is called "missing") and sometimes has thirty days (this type of month is considered "full").

The whys of a lunar calendar are just about as simple as its hows. Over the course of a month, the moon grows brighter and brighter, and then it grows dimmer and dimmer. This cycle of going from bright to dark to invisible and then becoming bright again is like the history of the Jewish people, a nation that has had some wonderfully bright times and some incredibly dark times. God therefore tells the Jewish people to count their months and years by the moon to remind them that just like the moon, they will never disappear forever.

There is an equally important message for us as individuals. When God instructs the Jewish people to count their months and years using the moon, He gives them an additional commandment: he tells them to "sanctify" the moon.

"Sanctify" is an interesting word. It means to set something apart in order to make it special. The idea of setting aside a place to be used for worship (like the mishkan) and thus making it special was not a new idea. Many ancient people had sanctified or holy places. The same was true of things, such as money or building materials or even animals to be sacrificed: they were set aside and dedicated to God.

Time is different. You cannot feel it or touch it. But with the commandment to sanctify the moon, God lets the Jewish people know that time can be sanctified just like places and things. (The best example of time being set aside and sanctified is the Sabbath day.) So perhaps God is telling us with the commandment of the lunar calendar that we should always try to "sanctify" our time, that is, to make it special.

Some people sanctify time with Bible study, and that is what you are doing right now by reading this book. Some sanctify time by helping others or by doing volunteer work. Spending quality time with your family or connecting with your parents or your siblings can even be thought of as sanctifying time.

The question is, how do any of us spend our free time? Many spend their free time on things like Instant Messenger, Twitter, Snapchat, or the latest game craze on their phones. And these are, it could be argued, examples of "unsanctifying" time. Some might even consider these to be examples of time lost that can't ever be recaptured.

So here is the lesson the moon teaches us as individuals. Yes, we can and sometimes do waste time or use it unwisely, which in a way is a bit like the dark phases of the moon. But like the moon, we can turn bright again by sanctifying our time and using it more productively.

> *List some of the ways you spend your free time. These may be fun, but are they productive? Are they sanctified? Why or why not? And if not, can you think of some new things you could do with your free time that would be "sanctified" or that would help you balance out your "sanctified" and "unsanctified" time?*

Making Life Cycle Events Meaningful

You may not use the term "life cycle events," but you surely know what they are: things like birthdays and your parents' anniversary, things that celebrate milestones in individual people's lives.

Without a doubt, these are important, but there are also life cycle events that mark milestones for a community or even a country—days like Thanksgiving and the Fourth of July. Days like these allow us to develop family traditions that add to the celebration. Maybe it's your grandmother's special stuffing recipe to go along with the turkey, or maybe it's the apple pie you eat every year while your family watches the fireworks display. Communal celebrations help us remember important events in our history but also allow us to add to them in ways that make them our own.

God certainly understands this when He commands the Jews while they are still slaves to celebrate their exodus from Egypt "all the days of your life." Jewish families around the world do this each year on the first nights of the Passover holiday by hosting a "seder." (No ritual is more widely observed among Jewish families than the Passover seder.)[1] At the seder, families read about the Exodus. They sing songs. They eat special foods, like matzah and bitter herbs. But

---

1. Feldman, "Odd and Instructive Habits."

the truth is, no two seders are exactly alike, even though families recite the same prayers and sing the same songs from a special book called the haggadah. Each family adds its own special element to make its seder unique. Maybe this involves special decorations for the table, or maybe it's a special, secret ingredient in the matzah balls in the chicken soup. Some families use fresh horseradish for their bitter herbs, while others use Romaine lettuce (yes, Romaine lettuce is considered a "bitter herb" at the seder). Some families even put small bags on their shoulders and march around the table to reenact the experience of leaving Egypt as free men and women.

All this should be a reminder that while ice cream and birthday cakes are great, memories and family traditions are even better.

Which of your family life cycle gatherings do you like best? Why? Do you think you will continue to have such gatherings when you have your own family? Why or why not?

Being Proud but Respectful

The tenth and final plague, the killing of all the firstborn in Egypt, is so terrible that Pharaoh gets up in the middle of the night and summons Moses to his palace. "Leave, go, get out! Take your people and go worship your God." These are Pharaoh's orders, and the Egyptian people agree. They urge their Jewish neighbors to hurry up and pack. And we know that the newly freed slaves are so rushed that their dough doesn't have time to rise, and so they leave Egypt with no real bread, only matzah.

Still, there are lots of Jews and lots of packing to do. It takes all night and most of the morning. And this week's reading makes special note of the time of day when they finally leave Egypt: midday. Does this detail strike you as odd? Does it really matter exactly what time the Jews left Egypt? Why does the text seem to go out of its way to mention this?

Good questions. To answer them, we need to see whether there are any other examples of the exact time of day being mentioned in a biblical story. There are two other well-known examples, and both come from the book of Genesis.

We find the first in the story of Noah and the great flood. Noah spends 120 years building the ark, and when the rains finally begin to fall and he and his family finally must enter the ark, we are told that they do this at "midday." Why midday? The people who mocked Noah all through the many years it took to build the ark now want to keep him and his family from entering it. God tells Noah to go in at midday, a time when everyone will see what's happening, as a sign to these people that there is nothing they can do to prevent this or to prevent the rains from falling and falling and falling.

The second example involves Abraham's circumcision ceremony. If you recall, God tells Abraham to circumcise himself (which involves cutting the foreskin off the tip of his penis) when he is ninety-nine years old. Abraham decides to host a party to celebrate his circumcision. And what time does this party start? Midday. Why? Abraham isn't concerned that his friends and neighbors will think he's crazy to do such a painful thing—especially at the age of ninety-nine! He doesn't hide his willingness to obey the command of God. Rather, he celebrates it in a very public manner (although the procedure itself is done in private).

How do these two other examples help us understand the Jews leaving Egypt at midday?

The Jews were enslaved for many years.[2] Pharaoh refused for the longest time to let them go, but in the end, the Egyptians have no other option. And the Jews leave at midday as a sign to the Pharaoh and his people that they are now powerless to stop this exodus.

But there is something else going on here, too. The Jews are happy—very, very happy—to finally be free. It would have been understandable for these former slaves to show their anger and bitterness. But they don't, because they have seen how badly the Egyptians were punished and how badly they suffered. The Jews do not mock the Egyptians or gloat over their sufferings. They

---

2. Just how long is debated by the rabbis. One view is that they were slaves for 210 years. Another is that they were slaves for 400 years.

are grateful to finally be free but are saddened by the suffering of the Egyptians.[3]

Had the Jews left in the middle of the night, the Egyptians would not have seen this restraint shown by the Jews. By leaving at midday, the Jews can make clear that they are neither mocking the Egyptians nor gloating over their suffering. This is another reason why leaving at midday is important: so that the Jews can show the Egyptians that they are leaving in a respectful, dignified manner.

What can we learn from this?

There are times when it is okay (or even more than okay) to show off your pride in certain things you do. Let's say you score four goals in a soccer match. Wow, that would be something! You would feel proud of your accomplishment. But what if your team won the match by a score of ten to zero? Maybe the other team isn't so skilled, and so maybe your four goals seem less special. Now, what if your team had won by a score of one to nothing, and you scored the only goal? Which seems more impressive or more difficult?

The same would be true for a writing contest or an art competition. Having the winning entry when only five people participate is different from winning when there are fifty entries.

The point is this: If you think carefully about your accomplishments and the context in which you achieve them, you can still feel proud, as you should. But context will help manage your enthusiasm and help you be mindful of the feelings of others. It will help you not gloat or be overly braggy. The Hebrew slaves understand this, and by leaving at midday, they show how one can be proud and respectful at the same time.

> *Have you ever done something really special that made you feel very proud? How did you share this with your friends? Were you braggy or did you share your exciting news in a respectful manner?*
>
> *Has someone ever bragged too much to you? How did that make you feel? What could they have done differently?*

---

3. This feeling of sadness at the suffering of others explains the custom all Jews have at their seders to pour a little wine from their cups as the ten plagues are recited.

Beshalach

(Exod 13:17–17:16)

The Exodus from Egypt

Summary of This Week's Reading

You might think that after so many long years of enslavement, the Jews would be anxious to get to the land God promised their ancestors Abraham, Isaac, and Jacob. But God has other plans. He knows that if any of Egypt's neighboring nations attack the Jews (which, as we will see, one does), the people will be so frightened that they will want to return to Egypt as quickly as possible. For this reason, God leads them into the desert by a much longer route. God shows them the way during the day with a pillar of cloud and at night with pillar of fire.

What's even more surprising is that after the Jews have been travelling for a few days, God commands them to retrace their steps and head back to Yam Suf. Why does God do this? To make the Egyptians think the Jews are hopelessly lost, which would prompt the Egyptians to chase after them. And that is exactly what happens.

When the people see the approaching Egyptian army, they panic. They scream at Moses and accuse him of taking them out of Egypt only to die in the desert. "Don't be afraid," Moses reassures them. "Stand firm and see how God will fight for you and save you."

Despite Moses's words, the people are frozen with fear. They refuse to move. God tells Moses to stretch out his staff over the sea and divide it and that once the sea is split, the Jews should march ahead, between the walls of water.

While this conversation is going on between God and Moses, Pharaoh and his soldiers are coming closer and closer. To protect the Jewish people, God places the pillar of cloud that normally leads the Jews between them and the Egyptians. Knowing that his people are safe, Moses stretches out his staff, and the sea splits. The people move ahead on the dry seabed.

At this point, God removes the pillar of cloud, as if to invite the Egyptians to chase after the Jews, and they quickly do. But Moses again stretches his hand over the sea, and the waters that had been standing like walls now fall upon the Egyptians, drowning them all. Moses and his sister Miriam lead the people in a song of praise, thanking God for the wondrous miracle that has just taken place.

With the Egyptian army crushed, the people travel into the desert for three days without finding any water to drink. They finally arrive at a place called Marah, where there is water, but the water is too bitter to drink. At the command of God, Moses throws a piece of wood into the water, which then becomes sweet enough to drink. (We will talk more about this shortly.)

A month goes by, and the Jews are running out of food. They complain to Moses and tell him that life was better for them in Egypt! In response, God tells Moses to inform the people that He, God, will rain down bread from heaven each morning and will provide them with meat every night. The meat, in the form of quails, appears in the evening and covers the camp. In the morning, this heavenly bread—called manna—covers the ground and is protected by layers of dew.

It is important to know that the manna is a kind of test for the Jewish people. Each person is to collect a set amount each morning for himself or herself—no more and no less. Plus, they are not to save any to eat the next day. This means that the people wake up each morning knowing that the only food they will have to eat that day will come from God. Almost everyone has faith in God, and they don't try to save any manna for the next day, which means that they pass the test.

Unfortunately, a few are not so strong. They ignore God's instructions, and when they awake the next day, the manna they saved is covered with worms, which, we can all agree, is pretty gross.

The instructions for Fridays are different. On Friday, everyone is to collect a double portion, one for Friday and another for the Sabbath, because no manna will fall on the Sabbath. Sadly, there are once again people who will not or cannot follow the directions of Moses. They go out on the Sabbath to look for manna but find none. God, of course, isn't too happy with these people.

The Jewish people travel further into the desert, and by the time they reach a place called Rephidim, they are again out of water. Not surprisingly, the people complain, and God hears their complaints. He tells Moses to hit a certain rock with his staff. Water miraculously comes pouring out of the rock, and the people drink.

This would be a nice, happy ending to this week's reading, but the story continues. Soldiers from a nation called Amalek show up and attack the Jews. (They focus their attack on the old, weak, and helpless, who travel slowly and trail behind.) Moses tells his student Joshua to assemble an army and go out to war against Amalek. Joshua does so, and the Jews are victorious, aided by a prayer Moses offers from the top of a mountain overlooking the battle. Once the battle is over, God tells Moses that "I will utterly blot out the memory of Amalek from under heaven!"

While we are not sure exactly where Mt. Sinai was located, here is the route the Jews most likely traveled when leaving Egypt.

Life Lessons from *Beshalach*

Sometimes in our weekly readings, the life lessons to be learned are rather obvious, but there are other times when our life lessons are less clear and require a bit of thought or explanation. We have both types in this week's reading, so let's start with the obvious and work our way up to the less obvious.

"Why Do You Cry Out to Me?"

Picture the scene. The Jews have left Egypt, thinking that they are at last free, both from slavery and from the cruelties of Pharaoh.

But they're not. No sooner do the former slaves leave Egypt than Pharaoh has a change of heart. "What is this we have done," Pharaoh cries out to his advisors, "releasing Israel from our service?"

Quickly, Pharaoh personally leads six hundred of his finest chariots in pursuit of Moses and the Jewish people, and the rest of Egypt's chariots are not far behind. When the Jews see this terrifying sight, they think they are going to die in the desert. They scream, "What have you done to us, taking us out of Egypt?" They cry out to Moses and even mock him, "Were there not enough graves in Egypt that you brought us to die in the wilderness?"

Moses tries to reassure the people. "Watch," he says, "and see what God will do the Egyptians." He tells them that God will save them, just as He saved them from slavery in Egypt. Then Moses does something very natural to him. He prays to God.

Makes sense, right? The Jewish people are trapped between the Egyptian chariots chasing them and Yam Suf (which, as we have already explained, is often mistranslated as the "Red Sea" instead of its correct meaning, the "Sea of Reeds"). Why wouldn't Moses turn to God in prayer? Why wouldn't he expect God to answer his prayers, just like God did in Egypt?

Surprisingly, God is not interested in prayer, at least not at this time. He says to Moses, "Why do you cry out to Me? Tell the Israelites to go forward."

It seems clear what God is telling Moses (and us, too) by not answering his prayer. Praying to God is a worthwhile and important thing to do. But simply praying, without taking any action yourself, is not what God wants from us. He wants and expects us to do what we can in life.

Think about it this way. Suppose you have a big math or science or English test. Your teacher gives you the worksheet, and you say a little prayer: "Please, God, let me do well on this test." If that is all you did, meaning, you pinned your hopes of getting a good grade on this short prayer without having studied the night before, you will probably do poorly on the test. It's not that God doesn't hear your prayer. He just doesn't answer it, and why should He? You did nothing to help yourself succeed.

If you can easily do something on your own, should you also pray to God for help? Or would it be better to finish up and then offer a prayer of thanks to God? Or do you think that when it comes to simple things, there is no need to pray to God? How are we to know when to turn to God and what to ask for?

Life's Natural Reactions Don't Reflect a Lack of Faith

After God splits Yam Suf and saves the Jews, they travel into the desert. They journey for three days without finding any water. Imagine their excitement when they arrive at a place called Marah and find water there! However, their excitement quickly changes to disappointment and even fear when they discover that the water is too bitter to drink.[1] They cry out to Moses, "What shall we drink?"

Wait a minute. After seeing the ten wondrous plagues God brought down on the Egyptians, after watching Him miraculously split the sea, how could the people doubt that God would once again work a miracle and provide them with water to drink? Shouldn't God be angry with the people for having so little faith in Him?

These are good questions, but the truth is, God doesn't get angry. He simply tells Moses to throw a piece of wood into the water.[2] Once Moses does this, the water becomes sweet, and the people have plenty to drink.

Here we have one of the less obvious lessons we referred to earlier.

Three days in the desert with no water? Of course the people are scared. Of course they're worried. It is only natural to be worried

1. The name of this place, Marah, means "bitter" in Hebrew.

2. At first glance, this seems like a miracle. However, some argue that it wasn't. Why? God surely had other means of making the water sweet. Instead, He told Moses to throw a particular kind of wood into the water, and this was because God wanted to teach Moses some common chemistry. By telling Moses to use this wood, God shows him how to use natural products to sweeten something that only needs sweetening in order to make it drinkable or edible.

under such circumstances, and God understands this. Being frightened or scared or nervous when it is perfectly natural to be frightened or scared or nervous is okay. It doesn't mean that we doubt God or lack faith in God. It just means that we are reacting as normal people do. And because the reactions of the people to their lack of water are so normal, God does what He normally does for the people. He helps them and gives them the water they need.

We see from this story that God doesn't expect us to be robot-like and never show our emotions. He expects us to be human, and humans can be nervous and concerned about something and still have faith in God that things will work out.

> Can you remember something that made you or your parents very worried and concerned? Did you think things would work out, or were you convinced that you and your family were "doomed"? Why did you feel this way? How did things work out in the end?

The Challenge of Being Different

Unfortunately, we live in a time in which it can be difficult to be different. People are sometimes teased or bullied or worse because of things that make them different, whether it's the color of their skin, their accent, their body type (being thought of as "too thin" or "too fat"), their hair, or any number of other characteristics.

Being a person of faith, being one who believes in God, can also make you seem different, and the Jewish people know all too well the price of being different.

If you think this is something new or something that only started in modern times, you need look no further than this week's reading to see that's not true. Not long after the Jewish people leave Egypt and cross Yam Suf, they are attacked by soldiers from the nation of Amalek. The story gives us no reason for the attack. The Jews are nowhere near Amalek. They pose no threat to Amalek. Amalek attacks the Jews because—well, just because. Or perhaps more correctly, Amalek attacks because the Jews are different. And what makes them so different? They believe in the one, true God, and they are proud of their belief.

Moses and the Jewish people of course fight back and defend themselves. They have no other choice. But if you are ever teased or made fun of just because you are different, you do have choices. You can politely ask the other person to stop. You can tell the other person how what he or she is doing makes you feel (probably bad, right?). You can tell your teachers or your parents about it and ask for their help.

Unlike the Jewish people when they were attacked by Amalek, your first choice if you are ever teased should not be to fight back. But this does not mean that you cannot or should not defend yourself if someone is hitting you or trying to physically hurt you.

We learn an important lesson from this story of Amalek. Like the Jews in desert, we should never be ashamed of those things that make us different or unique. We should be proud of who we are and of the things we believe in. And we should always stand up for ourselves when others tease or make fun of us—well, just because.

> *Have you ever been bullied or teased because you were different? What did you do about it? After reading the story of Amalek and thinking about it, could you have done something different to stop the teasing? What and why?*
>
> *Have you ever bullied someone? Why? How do you think your bullying made him or her feel? How did it make you feel?*

Yitro

(Exod 18:1–20:23)

Part One (for Parents and Educators)—Commandments or Utterances: What's the Difference?

You may have already learned what a synonym is: a word or phrase that means exactly or nearly the same thing as another word or phrase. Take the word "good." Synonyms for "good" include "excellent," "positive," and "first-class."

Hebrew is no different from English when it comes to synonyms, and remembering this will help us better understand this week's reading. Here's why.

There are a number of English translations for what God tells us to do in the Bible—big, fancy words like "testimonies" and "statutes." But the most commonly used word is "commandment" (*mitzvah* in Hebrew). If you are starting to wonder why this is beginning to sound like an English lesson, don't. All this talk about synonyms is important because this week's reading contains what are usually called the "Ten Commandments."

The Ten Commandments make up one of the best-known portions of the Torah. Movies have been made about them. People have had big fights over the years about where and how to display them in government buildings and other public places. The one thing people don't argue about is the name "Ten Commandments." But they should, because this name, in the original Hebrew, doesn't contain the word "commandments" at all. It doesn't even use a synonym for commandments!

How this incorrect translation became so commonly used isn't so important, but whether or not this section of the Torah actually contains ten commandments is. So let's take a closer look at the actual language of the verses.

What people commonly call the Ten Commandments begin with this verse: "God spoke all these words, saying." Not commandments. Words. And the first words Gods says (or "utters") after this introduction are: "I the LORD am your God who brought you out of the land of Egypt, the house of bondage."

Look closely at this sentence. Is God telling us to do anything? No. He is simply stating a fact: I, God, took the Jewish people out of Egypt and out of slavery.

Even though this sentence is not a commandment, Judaism counts it as one of the ten, and that's why Judaism doesn't call them the "Ten Commandments" but rather the "Ten Sayings" or the "Ten Utterances." ("Sayings" and "utterances" are synonyms.) In other words, in this section, God says ten very important things. Some of these are actually commandments, like "observe the Sabbath" and "honor your parents," but others are not.

All the various denominations of Christianity, from Catholics to Protestants, agree with Judaism's count: there are ten. But Christianity insists that these are ten commandments, not sayings. So what does Christianity do with the sentence about God taking the Jews out of Egypt? It is clearly *not* a commandment, so Christianity drops it from the list.

What a minute. If you drop one, you're left with nine, not ten! That's true, and that's why Christianity's counting of the Ten Commandments is different from Judaism's Ten Utterances, as you can see in the table below. Here's how it works: What Judaism counts as the first saying, Christianity excludes from its list. One approach to get to ten is to take the second one, which bans the worship of idols, and make it two commandments: you may not worship idols, and you may not even make idols. There is also another approach. Number ten in the Jewish count says: "You shall not covet ["covet" means to want something so badly that you will do almost anything to get it] your neighbor's house: you shall not covet your neighbor's wife, or his male or female slave, or his ox or his ass, or anything that is your neighbor's." This is a long saying (one that actually contains a commandment), and so the Catholic Church makes it two: you must not really, really want your neighbor's wife, and you must not really, really want your neighbor's house.

Ten Utterances	Ten Commandments 1	Ten Commandments 2
1. I am the Lord Your God . . .		
2. You shall have no other gods before Me . . . You shall not make images	1. You shall have no other gods before Me . . . 2. You shall not make images	1. You shall have no other gods before Me . . . You shall not make images
3. You shall not take the name of the Lord . . .	3. You shall not take the name of the Lord . . .	2. You shall not take the name of the Lord . . .
4. Remember the Sabbath . . .	4. Remember the Sabbath . . .	3. Remember the Sabbath . . .
5. Honor your father and mother.	5. Honor your father and mother.	4. Honor your father and mother.
6. You shall not murder.	6. You shall not murder.	5. You shall not murder.
7. You shall not commit adultery.	7. You shall not commit adultery.	6. You shall not commit adultery.
8. You shall not steal.	8. You shall not steal.	7. You shall not steal.

Ten Utterances	Ten Commandments 1	Ten Commandments 2
9. You shall not bear false witness.	9. You shall not bear false witness.	8. You shall not bear false witness.
10. You shall not covet . . .	10. You shall not covet . . .	9. You shall not covet your neighbor's house.
		10. You shall not covet your neighbor's wife.

The bottom line is this: all the religions whose belief in God is based on the Bible—Judaism, Christianity, and Islam—recognize that this is a very, very important section of the Bible, no matter what you call it. The difference between "commandments" and "utterances" simply comes down to how you count and group these verses from the book of Exodus.

Yitro

(Exod 18:1–20:23)

Part Two—Revelation

Summary of This Week's Reading

Jethro (Yitro in Hebrew), the father of Moses's wife Zipporah, hears the amazing tales of what God has done for the Jewish people when freeing them from slavery in Egypt. Something in these stories makes him decide to leave Midian and go find Moses and his people in the Sinai Desert. When Jethro finally arrives, Moses greets him warmly and then tells him the details of all God has done to the Egyptians. Jethro thanks God for all the miracles and even offers thanksgiving sacrifices!

During his time with the Jewish people in the desert, Jethro sees that in addition to teaching the people about the laws of God, Moses serves as judge when people have legal questions or disputes. The problem is that Moses is spending hours and hours each day judging cases, which means that people are standing in line for hours and hours each day waiting for their turn to present their case. Jethro suggests that Moses create a system of judges to help him. "What a great idea!" says Moses, and so he creates a system of courts. Some judges are responsible for smaller groups (numbering from ten to fifty), while others have much larger groups to deal with (from hundreds to thousands).

Having brought Zipporah back to her husband and having helped Moses solve a very big problem, Jethro decides to return home to Midian.

At this point in the story, it has been six weeks since the Jewish people left Egypt. They are now at Mount Sinai. The people remain at the foot of the mountain while Moses climbs up to receive a message from God for the people. Part of the message is that the Jewish people are to be role models for humanity. How so? By following the laws of the Torah and being kind, honest, caring, and charitable toward others in addition to believing in the one, true God, the Jewish people can show the world how truly great human beings can be.

Three days pass, as the people prepare themselves for a "face-to-face" encounter with God. Of course, they do not see God, because God has no physical form. But on the morning of the third day, there is much for them to see and hear. Thunder and lightning fill the sky. A thick cloud covers the top of Mount Sinai. A piercing sound of a ram's horn is heard from the mountaintop. The people are frightened. They stand shuddering, but Moses brings them close to the base of the mountain.

It is now time for God to come down to the top of the mountain and for Moses to go up there to meet Him. God speaks ten utterances, which teach the people many important lessons—things like believing in God, keeping the Sabbath, and honoring parents. There are also things we must never do, like murder, steal, or tell lies about another person in court. (According to the rabbinic tradition, the lessons in the Ten Utterances were meant for all people, not just the Jews.)

It is hard to describe just what really goes on during these moments at Mount Sinai. But whatever it is, it leaves the people shaken. They ask Moses if, from now on, he could bring the word of God to them, because hearing the word of God from God Himself is too intense an experience. Moses agrees to their request.

Life Lessons from *Yitro*

God's revelation at Mount Sinai and His giving the Ten Utterances (along with all the other commandments of the Torah) to the Jewish people is such an important event that it can be easy to forget about anything else that happens in this week's reading. But lots of other things do take place in this reading, and many of them involve Jethro, after whom the parasha is named. There are some important life lessons we can learn from his actions.

Knowing Why Can Make a Difference

This week's reading begins by telling us that Jethro hears something that prompts him to take his daughter Zipporah (who happens to be Moses's wife) and her two sons to the Sinai Desert so they can be reunited with Moses and the Jewish people. (Moses leaves his family behind in Midian when he goes to confront Pharaoh in Egypt at the command of God.) The story does not tell us exactly what he hears or why it makes him want to seek out the Jewish people in the Sinai Desert. It simply says that Jethro goes.

One would think that Jethro bringing Zipporah and her sons to rejoin the Jewish people is a good thing, so why should we care about the reasons behind it? Isn't the outcome what really matters?

Maybe here, where the outcome is so positive, the reasons why it happens are less important. But this is not always true. When we understand why a person does something, it makes it easier for us to be more sympathetic or more understanding of the results of his or her actions. It makes it harder for us to judge or second guess their actions.

This story about Jethro gives us a good example of how knowing the reason for an action can make a big difference in how we react to that action.

The rabbinic tradition suggests that Jethro hears about two things before deciding to go to Moses in the desert. One is the war with Amalek, and the other is the splitting of Yam Suf. The question is, which of these really prompts him to act?

The news of the war with Amalek worries Jethro, because God declared in last week's reading that He would wage war against Amalek forever. Jethro lives in Midian, which is close to where the people of Amalek live. He is worried that when the war comes, he and his family will be harmed by it. For him, the smart decision is to leave and bring Zipporah back to Moses. If he stays with Moses, he will certainly be safe. And should he decide to return to Midian (which he does), Jethro can remind the Jewish soldiers fighting against Amalek that he, Jethro, is family, even if he himself isn't actually Jewish.

The splitting of Yam Suf impacts Jethro in a different way. Jethro knows that Moses has left his wife behind in Midian. He may even have divorced her! (It's not that Moses doesn't love his wife or his children, but rather, all his attention and energy are focused on serving God and the Jewish people.) When Jethro hears about the splitting of the sea, he has an insight into the marriage of Moses and Zipporah. Jethro thinks, Even though the waters of the sea are split apart, God brings them back together again, and this is like the situation of Moses and Zipporah. Their marriage has been split apart, but maybe when Jethro brings

Zipporah back to Moses, they can be reunited with God's help, just as God reunited the waters of Yam Suf.

What do we see? The first explanation, that Jethro goes to Moses because of the war with Amalek, suggests that Jethro is thinking about himself and his own safety. The second explanation, that it is the splitting of the sea that prompts him to go, suggests that he is concerned for his daughter. In either case, Jethro goes to the Sinai Desert and brings Zipporah with him. But these two possible explanations for why he goes make us look at Jethro and this story very differently. The first explanation makes us think that Jethro may be self-centered and only worried about himself. The second instead makes us see Jethro as a caring and concerned father.

Which version of Jethro is the more sympathetic character? The second one, for sure.

> *When your friends or family members do something, do you ever stop and ask them why? Can you remember a time when knowing why they did something made you look at their actions differently? How so?*

He is Everyone's God[1]

A second lesson we learn from Jethro in this week's reading may seem a little surprising to some, but it shouldn't. Jethro shows us that God is not just the God of the Jewish people. He is God to all who choose to believe in Him.

To better understand this, we need to examine a longstanding custom among the Jewish people. For centuries, when someone would ask a Jew, "How are you?," he or she would answer with the Hebrew phrase *Baruch Hashem*, which means "Thank God" or "Blessed be the Lord." It didn't matter whether the person was rich or poor, healthy or sick. The response would always be "Thank God."

---

1. This life lesson is based on an article on this week's reading by former chief rabbi of Great Britain, Rabbi Jonathan Sacks, entitled "The Universal and the Particular," which he posted to his website (http://rabbisacks.org/covenant-conversation-homepage/) in 2020.

This is, of course, a response that shows faith in God and in all that He does. What is interesting is that the source for this custom in the Torah comes from people who aren't Jewish!

The first person to offer praise to God is Noah, who, when he pays tribute to his son, proclaims: "Blessed be the LORD, the God of Shem." The second is Abraham's servant Eliezer, who, after successfully finding a wife for his master's son, declares: "Blessed be the LORD, the God of my master Abraham, who has not withheld His steadfast faithfulness from my master."

And then there is Jethro. When he arrives at Mount Sinai (along with Zipporah and her children), he is greeted warmly by Moses, who proceeds to tell Jethro all the details of the wondrous things God has done for the Jewish people, both in Egypt with the plagues and at Yam Suf. Jethro may not be Jewish and may not have shared in the sufferings of the Jewish people, but he recognizes the greatness of God. He is moved to praise the one, true God he believes in: "Blessed be the LORD (*Baruch Hashem*) who delivered you from the Egyptians and from Pharaoh and who delivered the people from under the hand of the Egyptians."

It is true that God reveals Himself with thunder and lightning to the Jewish people at Mount Sinai, where He Himself speaks the Ten Utterances. He there gives the Jewish people a special mission, to be a role model for all humanity. But being a role model on behalf of God only makes sense if God does not limit His grace and kindness to the Jewish people.[2] This is precisely what Jethro teaches us when he says, "Blessed be the LORD (*Baruch Hashem*)." A line from the biblical book of Psalms summarizes this idea: "The LORD is near to all who call Him, to all who call Him with sincerity."

Noah sought God with sincerity, as did Eliezer and Jethro—as have countless numbers of people, Jews and non-Jews alike, since

---

2. This concept, that God is a God to all people, is a major theme of the Jewish prayer services on Rosh Hashanah, the Jewish New Year. The prayer service specifically says, "As a shepherd herds his flock, causing his sheep to pass beneath his staff, so do You cause to pass, count, and record, visiting *the souls of all living*, decreeing the length of their days, inscribing their judgment."

God appeared to humanity at Mount Sinai. In this week's reading, Jethro reminds us that God is the God of all humanity.

> *If you think about it, Jews, Christians, and Muslims all believe in the same God. They just have different ways of worshipping Him. Should this matter? Does it matter to you? Do you think it matters to God?*

Knowing When to Ask For Advice or Help

Moses is a pretty special person. God chooses him to lead the Jewish people out of Egypt. He alone goes up Mount Sinai to speak, as the story tells us, "face-to-face" with God. (No one is quite sure exactly how that worked.) God reveals His entire code of laws to Moses, who will spend the next forty years teaching these laws to the Jewish people. But even someone as bright and talented and special as Moses needs help or advice from time to time, as we see in this week's reading.

After spending a little time with Moses, Jethro notices that the people come to him from morning to evening "to inquire of God." Moses is patient. He gives the people the time they need to present their cases and to ask their questions, but this goes on for hours. Moses barely has time to do anything else, and the same is true for the people who stand in line all day waiting for a chance to ask their questions. Moses thinks he has no choice but to answer all these questions himself, but Jethro tells him: "The thing you are doing is not right; you will surely wear yourself out, and these people as well."

Moses immediately recognizes that Jethro is correct. When Jethro gives him advice on how to fix the situation, suggesting that he create a system of judges, Moses quickly agrees to put the plan into place.

This is the third very important life lesson we learn from Jethro. No matter how smart a person is, no matter how good he or she is at something, they can always benefit from good advice offered by others. A wise person understands this, and Moses, as we all know, is a very wise person indeed.

Are you the type of person who accepts advice from others? Do you react differently when you ask someone for his or her help compared to when these same people offer help without asking if you need or want it? If the person offers good advice or help that you need, should this matter?

Mishpatim

(Exod 21:1–24:18)

More Than Ten

Summary of This Week's Reading

While the laws set forth in this week's reading seem to be separate from the revelation at Mount Sinai, they are not. All the laws here are given by God to Moses at Mount Sinai, just as the Ten Utterances were given to the Jewish people at Mount Sinai.

The reading begins with what we would call "civil laws," or laws that cover behavior and business dealings between people. The first of these civil laws relates to Jewish "slaves." They are not slaves in the sense that we think of when we study U.S. history, particularly the period before and during the Civil War. Rather, this kind of "slave" is someone who owes money to someone else but isn't able to repay their debt. They must therefore work for the other person until the debt is paid off or until they have completed six years of service, whichever comes first. (This helps explain why the text calls these people "slaves" even though they are not slaves in the usual sense of the word. The Hebrew word for slave, eved, comes from the Hebrew word for "to work," la'avod.) Other laws in this section include punishments for murder, kidnapping, and abusing one's parents.

The next set of laws covers the penalties for a person who injures another, including specific punishments for one who kills or injures his servant and for one who causes a woman to miscarry. There is a related discussion about the punishments a person faces if his or her animals damage another person's property.

The focus of the laws then shifts to theft. The text teaches us that someone who steals must pay for what he or she stole, plus a fine. While on the topic of stealing, there is a discussion of a person's right to self-defense if a thief tries to rob him or her.

The rest of the civil laws presented here cover a wide range of very different things, from the punishment an arsonist faces for damages caused by fires that he or she ignites to prohibitions against bullying a foreigner, widow, or orphan. We learn about the commandment to lend money to the poor as well as the prohibition against lending with interest to other Jews. There are also commandments to return a lost animal to its owner and to help unload an overburdened animal. (In a society in which almost everyone is a farmer, these are very important laws.)

Once the sections on civil law are complete, we turn to ritual laws, which have to do with religious observances. The commandment of Shemitah (the Sabbatical Year) is the first to be introduced: we are allowed to work and harvest the land for six years, and on the seventh year we let the land rest. We have the commandment to celebrate the three major pilgrimage festivals—Passover, Shavuot (Pentecost in English), and Sukkot (Tabernacles in English)—by traveling to the holy temple in Jerusalem. Finally, there is one of the core principles of the Jewish dietary laws: not to cook meat in (its mother's) milk.

After giving the Jewish people this very large and diverse group of laws, God tells them that He will send an angel to lead them into the land of Canaan. If they faithfully follow the lead of this angel, says God, the Jewish people will be rewarded. The enemies they will encounter in Canaan will fall before them, and God will greatly bless the Jews.

The reading concludes by telling us about some of the events that occur in the days just prior to God speaking to the Jews on Mount Sinai. Moses goes up the mountain and receives a message from God to be delivered to the people. The people in turn enthusiastically commit themselves to following all of God's laws. Then, together with the firstborn, Moses offers sacrifices to seal the covenant the Jewish people have made with God. Lastly, we read about God summoning Moses—after the giving of the Ten Utterances—to go up the mountain, where he will remain for forty days and nights, after which he will return to the people with the tablets.

Life Lessons from *Mishpatim*

Just Because

Have your parents ever told you to do something "just because"? How did that make you feel? Confused? Frustrated? Believe it or not, God sometimes does the same thing. Sometimes He commands us to do something "just because." Here's how this works:

There are a number of ways to think about the commandments in the Torah. A simple one is that there are positive commandments (the kind that tell us *to* do something) and negative ones (the kind that tell us *not* to do something).

A less obvious but equally important way to think about commandments has to do with how easily they are understood. What does this mean? Simply this: There are lots of commandments that need little or no explanation, like the commandments not to murder or steal. Everyone can agree that murder and stealing are bad things, and that is why we refer to such commandments as "common-sense laws." Common-sense laws are usually things people would have decided to do or not to do even if God had not given us commandments about them. (At least, this is how we like to think of them, but more on this shortly.)

The Torah also has a number of commandments that don't make much sense at all, and for this reason, we call them "non-common-sense laws." For example, Jews are prohibited from wearing garments made out of a combination of wool and linen (something called *shatnez* in Hebrew). It's not that God's fashion sense is somehow offended by people wearing wool and linen together. This law exists just because God says so. Another excellent example is the Jewish dietary laws. Is there any good reason why Jews should only eat the meat of animals that have split hoofs and chew their cud?[1] Is there any good reason why Jews should only eat fish that have fins and scales? No, there isn't. Then why do the Jewish people follow these rules? Just because God says so!

All this brings up an important question. We can accept things that God commands us "just because," even if we don't know their reason. That is what people of faith who wish to serve the one, true God do. But why give us commandments that are obvious and make sense? Why command us about things we could have figured out on our own?

The answer is that things we humans think are obvious are not always so obvious. Take murder as an example. You live in a country where it is obvious that murder is wrong. But in certain countries (such as Pakistan), though it is still against the law, it is not so obvious to people that murder is always wrong. In fact, in these countries, it is considered okay to kill a young woman who embarrasses her family by the clothing she chooses to wear or by marrying a man her father disapproves of.[2] This is why God gives us common-sense laws. By giving us common-sense laws, God is telling us that His commandments, whether they make sense or not, are to be followed because—well, just because. Just because this is what God wants us to do or not to do.

This is the most important life lesson to be learned from this week's reading. Our reading begins: "And these are the rules that you shall set before them." As we have seen before, the word "and" in the Torah can be very significant, and it is significant here. This "and" is teaching us that all the "rules" in this week's reading, many of which seem obvious and make a great deal of sense to us, are just as important as the Ten Utterances spoken by God Himself in last week's reading. In the end, there aren't really common-sense laws and non-common-sense laws. They are all simply God's laws.

1. When an animal chews its cud, it chews something, swallows it, brings it back up, and chews it a second time before swallowing it for good. This makes it easier for the animal to digest what it is eating. We all know that cows chew their cud, but so do camels and pigs.

2. According to Human Rights Watch, there are about 1,000 "honor kill-ings" in Pakistan every year. See Ijaz, "Pakistan Should Not Again."

At some point, your parents probably told you to do something "just because." Did you do what they asked, or did you first ask them for a better reason than "just because"? If you asked for a reason, why did you think they had to explain it to you before you did as they asked?

What I Said Isn't What I Meant

Have you ever said something to a friend that you thought was very clear, but somehow, your friend misunderstood what you meant? Maybe he didn't understand the words you used. Maybe she needed to be there to fully understand what was going on. In either case, what your friend heard was not at all what you meant or even what you thought you said.

When this happens to us, it is usually an accident. People generally try to say exactly what they mean. The same holds true for God. Throughout the Torah, God says what He means (and means what He says) over and over. But sometimes God says something that seems to mean one thing when it really means something else. Why He might do so is an important topic for us to consider, and in discussing it, we can learn something very significant about Jewish law.

When God gives His law to Moses, He gives Moses many commandments with all their details in writing. Others He gives to Moses in writing but with far fewer details. In order to avoid confusion among the Jewish people as to how these laws work, God also gives Moses verbal explanations. In short, some laws and details are given in writing, while others are only given verbally.

It isn't clear why God does this, but it is long established in the Jewish tradition that there is a Written Law (the laws as they are written in the Torah) and an Oral Law (the laws as Moses was told to explain them). And in this week's reading, we have one of the most famous examples of why both are needed.

Imagine that two people get into an argument. They get angrier and angrier with each other, until finally, the yelling stops and the punching and hitting begins. It's a bad fight, and one of them hits the other so hard that he or she is seriously hurt. What does Jewish law say about such a case? The language in the Written Law about this is shocking. It says that if one person hurts another, "the penalty shall be life for life, eye for eye, tooth for tooth, hand for hand, foot for foot, burn for burn, wound for wound, bruise for bruise."

Wow! These verses seem to be saying that if you were to hit a friend and knock out his tooth or break her arm, he would be allowed to knock out your tooth, and she would be allowed to break your arm. That seems crazy! And it would be crazy, if it were in fact the law. But here, what is written ("eye for eye, tooth for tooth") has a very different meaning when we look closely at the Oral Law.

The Oral Law makes clear why this idea of an eye for an eye cannot be taken literally. Here are two arguments that show why the Written Law in this case must mean something else:

> R. Shimon ben Yochai stated: "Eye for eye"—money. You say money; but perhaps it means literally an eye? In that case, if a blind man blinded another, a cripple maimed another, how would I be able to give an eye for an eye literally? Yet, the Torah states: "one law there shall be for you"—a law that applies equally to all of you!
>
> It was taught in the school of Hezekiah: "Eye for eye, life for life" and not a life and an eye for a life; for should you imagine it is literally meant [that you take out an eye for an eye], it would sometimes happen that an eye and a life would be taken for an eye, for in the process of blinding him, he might die [and then you have taken both his life and his eye, instead of just his eye].

Taken together, the Written and the Oral Law teach us two things: first, one pays a fine in cases of damages to another person, and second, the fine covers the money the hurt person lost from not working because of his injuries, plus the pain, emotional distress, and embarrassment suffered by the hurt person. So if the law as written isn't to be taken literally, why doesn't God simply say what He means?

When God gave His laws to the Jewish people at Mount Sinai, other nations already had their own sets of laws. At that time, in those other nations, the law in the case of damages to another person was literally "an eye for an eye." In other words, if you accidently poked out your friend's eye, he would get to poke out your eye! Things like this actually happened in some parts of the ancient world (like Babylonia). The Jewish people, who had lived in Egypt for so long, probably saw similarly harsh consequences as normal.[3]

The desire to hit back, to hurt another who has hurt you, is understandable. Everyone at some point has probably felt that way, if only for a minute. But "an eye for an eye?" That's cruel. That's harsh. And God certainly was not pleased that such things had become normal. One way to show the Jewish people that it was time for a "new normal" was to put this "foreign" law in writing but change it in the Oral Law to make it merciful. By doing so, God demonstrates that He plans on holding the Jewish people to a different and higher standard.

Today, when students read about the law of "eye for an eye" for the first time, they just know that something isn't quite right. They just know that Jewish law does not and cannot work this way, even if things like this were done at the time the Torah was given to the Jewish people. By writing it one way ("eye for an eye" in the Written Law) but explaining it in a different way ("money for an eye" in the Oral Law), God is doing two things. He is showing us that the ancient laws no longer apply for His people, and at the same time, He is forcing us to think very, very carefully about the law and exactly how it needs to work.

> *Sometimes, when people say or write something, they will go back and explain it again, just to be sure that everything is very clear. How would you say that having a Written and an Oral Law is meant to achieve this same goal?*

3. A common torture technique in ancient Egypt was beating the soles of the feet with a stick. Egyptians also used to smear disobedient slaves with ass's milk and seclude them until they had been thoroughly bitten by ants, fleas, and other insects. http://factsanddetails.com/world/cat56/sub404/entry-6143.html

Yes, Dignity for All

Of all the events of the six days of creation, perhaps the most dramatic is when God turns to the heavenly host and says: "Let us make man in our image, after our likeness." The rabbis of the Talmud struggled to explain the phrase "in our likeness." They knew that God has no body or physical form, so "in our likeness" cannot mean two eyes, two ears, two legs, and two arms. In the end, they concluded that "in our likeness" must mean that people should try to be like God by being kind, generous, and merciful. By being very patient. By helping those in need and by visiting the sick. By always striving to do good deeds.

When people act like God in these ways, they reflect the image of God, and they are to be respected, just like God is to be respected. God reminds us of this by commanding us to specifically honor certain individuals, like our parents and our teachers.

There is another concept that comes with being a reflection of the image of God. Human beings possess a certain amount of what we call "dignity." There are lots of definitions of this word. Some define dignity as showing respect for yourself in all areas: how you dress, how to speak to others, even how and what you eat. Others define it as having a noble character and a certain worthiness. Perhaps the best definition for the times we live in is this: dignity is the right of a person to be valued and respected for his or her own sake and to always be treated fairly and equally.

When you think about it, all this makes a great deal of sense. You certainly know many people who act in a dignified way and who deserve your respect. But maybe you can think of (or have heard about) people who don't act in ways deserving of respect. If so, must you respect them anyway? This week's reading answers that question for us with an unusual law about stealing.

In the system of laws we read about last week, there was no such thing as jail. If a person stole something, when he or she was caught, the stolen item had to be returned. Plus, the thief had to pay a fine to the owner of the stolen object. When it comes to stolen animals, the law is very, very specific: "When a man steals an ox or a sheep, and slaughters it or sells it, he shall pay five oxen for the ox, and four sheep for the sheep."

This seems confusing. If the purpose of the big fine is to keep people from stealing, why have different penalties for oxen and sheep? Here is a case where the midrash helps us understand what is really going on. The midrash points out that oxen are big and strong and can thus walk by themselves. Young sheep (the type a thief would most want to steal) are much smaller and weaker. Because of this, it is very likely that the thief would have to carry the young sheep on his or her shoulders. Carrying an animal like that is humiliating for the thief, and that is why (according to the midrash) God sets a lower fine for stealing sheep. It is as if God doesn't want to use punishment to further push down someone who already pushed himself down. It is as if God wishes to show respect to this person so as not to push him too far down.

Imagine that. Even thieves deserve a certain amount of respect. And that is the point. We might have thought that thieves, who are clearly doing bad things, don't deserve any respect. Not true. Thieves are still human beings, and all humans deserve a certain level of respect because thieves, like all people, are created in the image of God (even when they act like they don't remember it!).

> If you were to see someone doing something wrong, do you think it would be possible to show them a degree of respect without acting in a way that suggested that you agreed with what they were doing? What might that look like? Would it involve your actions or your speech?

Terumah

(Exod 25:1–27:19)

Part One (for Parents and Educators)—Why Sacrifice? Why Prayer?

Beginning with this week's reading, and for five weeks in total, we read about the construction of the tabernacle (*mishkan* in Hebrew, sometimes also called a "sanctuary" in English). There are many, many details recorded in these five weekly readings about the materials used to build the tabernacle as well as the people who assisted Moses in building it. More important, we read about how and when the tabernacle was used by the Jewish people to worship God, and worship in those days was all about animal sacrifices.

For us today, animal sacrifices seem strange and even cruel. We who pray to God find it hard to imagine why people ever sacrificed animals to God. It thus seems reasonable to ask, Why sacrifices? And when and why did people switch from sacrifices to prayer as we know it?

To answer these questions, we need to start with the earliest of stories in the Bible. We see that people, starting with the children of Adam and Eve, had a strong desire to thank and worship God. How did they do so? With sacrifices. "In the course of time, Cain brought an offering to the LORD from the fruit of the soil, and Abel, for his part, brought the choicest [the best] of the firstlings of his flock."

We see in this story of Cain and Abel the desire—or even need—of our earliest ancestors to offer thanks to God in the form of sacrifices. And people who remained devoted to God continued to use sacrifices to worship and give thanks for many centuries. For instance, take Noah. When Noah and his family finally leave the ark to rebuild civilization, what is Noah's first act? He builds an altar to God and offers burnt offerings on the altar, using the clean animals and clean birds that he brought with him on the ark.[1]

What about Abraham? Upon rediscovering and reintroducing God to the world, he also uses sacrifice to worship God, as the stories about him tell us on more than one occasion:

> The LORD appeared to Abram and said, "I will assign this land to your offspring." And he built an altar there [to offer a sacrifice] to the LORD who had appeared to him.
> From there he moved on to the hill country east of Bethel and pitched his tent, with Bethel on the west and Ai on the east; and he built there an altar [to offer a sacrifice] to the LORD and invoked the LORD by name.
> And Abram moved his tent, and came to dwell at the terebinths of Mamre, which are in Hebron; and he built an altar there [to offer a sacrifice] to the LORD.

Abraham's use of sacrifice doesn't mean that he doesn't also pray to God. In one instance, the Torah states very clearly that Abraham does just this: "Abraham then prayed to God, and God healed Abimelech and his wife and his slave girls, so that they bore children."

There's more. Our rabbis, in discussing why Jews must pray three times each day, tell us that "our forefathers instituted [that is, were the first to use] prayer, as the verse states: 'Next morning, Abraham hurried to the place where he had stood before the LORD.'" How do we know that Abraham is here praying to God? Simple. The Hebrew word for "stand" always represents prayer.

---

1. Remember that while Noah took two of all animals, male and female, with him into the ark, he made a point of taking seven pairs of clean animals and birds to be used as sacrifices to God.

That's not all. Not only was Abraham the first to offer morning prayers, but, according to these same rabbis, Isaac was the first to pray the afternoon prayers, and Jacob was the first to pray at night.

We know that Abraham, Isaac, and Jacob had very special relationships with God. They spoke with Him, they argued with Him, and they taught thousands of people to recognize and worship Him. And yes, at times, they even prayed to Him. Still, they usually worshipped and thanked Him through sacrifice.

With this as background, we can better understand the experiences of the generation that left Egypt and stood before God at Mount Sinai. The Jewish people came away from Mount Sinai with a system of sacrifices laid out in great detail. Like all the sacrifices offered to God before the giving of the law at Mount Sinai, these sacrifices were meant to be a way for the people to thank and worship God.

Was worship limited to sacrifice? No, not at all. The Jewish people prayed to God with songs of praise when they crossed Yam Suf: "Then Moses and the Israelites sang this song to the LORD." Their leaders, most notably King David, wrote songs of praise, which today serve as major parts of the Jewish prayer service. Still, these examples of song rather than sacrifice were the exception, not the rule. Sacrifice remained the primary form of Jewish worship for hundreds of years, from the days of Moses to the time of the First Temple itself.

This leaves us with a very big question: When did prayer replace sacrifice as the way of worshipping God and why? Answering this requires a brief history lesson.

With the destruction of the First Temple in the year 586 BCE and the exile of most Jews to Babylonia, there was a dramatic change in the relationship between the Jewish people and God. While the First Temple stood, God's Presence was literally visible. Holiness and prophecy were everywhere. One could go up to the Temple Mount and see miracles every day: the pillar of God's glory, the fire that came down from heaven, the smoke that went up from the altar (which, according to the midrash, appeared in the shape of a lion), and more.

Most important, sacrifice was, during this time, the basic way for the nation and for individuals to worship God. Prayer, if used at all, was a secondary and very personal way to worship.

Seventy years after the destruction of the First Temple, Daryavesh (Darius), the son of Esther and Achashverosh, granted the Jews permission to continue building a second temple in Jerusalem (construction had begun seventeen years earlier under the reign of Cyrus but was soon halted). Understandably, the Jewish people were anxious to regain what they had lost, so much so that even before completion of their new temple, daily sacrifices were begun anew.

The time of the Second Temple was an interesting one. True, the temple had been rebuilt, but it was impossible not to notice the changed relationship between God and the Jewish people. The Divine Presence didn't rest on the land of Israel as it had before the First Temple was destroyed. There was no prophecy and no holy ark in the temple, and many of the miracles that were present in the First Temple were gone.[2]

In short, the very strong and very real connection with God that was necessary for sacrifice to be the main way to worship and thank Him was no longer present.

As if in response, the Jewish sages introduced prayers into the sacrificial service during the time of the Second Temple. For instance, the priests who served in the temple and offered the daily sacrifices would recite some of the prayers that Jews say to this very day (such as the Shema and its blessings and the "sim shalom" blessing in the Amidah). On the Sabbath, they would add a blessing for the incoming watch of priests: "May He who has caused His name to dwell in this house cause to dwell among you love, brotherhood, peace, and friendship."

2. According to the Babylonian Talmud (Yoma 21b), these items and miraculous occurrences were present in the First Temple but absent in the Second: the ark of the covenant (which included the miraculous cherubs that were on the ark's cover); the heavenly fire; the Divine Presence; the Divine Spirit; and the *Urim VeTummim*.

Such changes were not limited to the priests and their service. The individuals who assisted the priests in the temple service played musical instruments and recited the daily psalm. Even those who didn't serve in the temple but merely came to Jerusalem to offer their own personal sacrifices would pray and read from the Torah after priests sacrificed the animals they had brought.

Important as these changes were, they were limited to the temple. What about the people's relationship with God? What could be done about that?

The great leader of this time, Ezra, understood the need to restore and even strengthen the people's connection with God. He realized that one way to do this would be to introduce formal and fixed public prayer.

Of course, as we have seen, prayer was not a new concept. It had been used by individuals and even the nation as a whole since the days of Abraham. However, those early prayers were not the same as the new prayers that Ezra required the people to say.

The prayers established by Ezra represented a completely new form of worship and expression, one made necessary by the Jewish people's loss of Hebrew as their common language during the exile that occurred after the destruction of the First Temple. This is understandable, as Jews were living all over the world, as they do today. As the rabbis of that time noted, "to recite the praises of the Holy One, blessed be He, in the holy language [i.e., Hebrew]" became an impossible task. For this reason, Ezra established eighteen mandatory benedictions, a group of blessings that ultimately came to be known as the Amidah. These prayers would be used by Jews no matter where they lived, and they would be said in Hebrew, so that Jews could pray together no matter what languages they spoke.

Ezra also decided that the number of times the Amidah should be said each day should equal the number of daily sacrifices that had been offered in the temple. This meant two prayer services every day (to match the two daily offerings brought in the temple each morning and afternoon). The people then decided that a third prayer should be said each day, at night, to match the time at which the limbs of the afternoon offerings were left to burn on the altar.

Given the destruction of the temple and the weakening of the people's connection to God that resulted, the rabbis' decision to link prayer to sacrifice is understandable. Prayer may have taken the place of sacrifice, but the strong desire to praise and worship God that made people long ago wish to offer sacrifices to God was not to be forgotten.

Terumah

(Exod 25:1–27:19)

Part Two—A Bit of Heaven on Earth

Summary of This Week's Reading

This is the first of five consecutive weekly readings about the construction of an earthly dwelling place for God's presence. In Hebrew, this structure is called the mishkan, *a word that is sometimes translated as "sanctuary" or "tabernacle."*

God commands the Jewish people to build Him a mishkan, but the construction process actually begins with a request. God tells Moses to ask the Jewish people to bring all the materials needed to build this sanctuary. He then gives Moses detailed instructions regarding the construction and dimensions of the sanctuary and its vessels, starting with the ark, which will hold the two stone tablets Moses brings down from Mount Sinai.

The ark is to be made of gold-plated acacia wood. Rings will be attached to the corners of the ark, and poles will be inserted into the rings when the ark is to be moved. Its cover is to be made from a slab of pure gold, and two angels, called cherubim, are to be placed on top of it, sitting face-to-face.

Next come the instructions for building a table for the showbread. (These are twelve loaves of bread, one for each tribe of the Jewish people, that are baked fresh each Friday and then placed in the mishkan, where they remain for an entire week.) This table is also to be made of gold-plated acacia wood, and it also has rings for the poles used to move it.

The seven-branched menorah (candelabra) is next on God's list. Like the top of the ark, it, too, is to be made of a single block of pure gold. It has decorative cups, knobs, and flowers on its body.

Now that God has explained to Moses how to build some of the most important vessels used in the mishkan, it is time for instructions for building the structure itself. It is important to remember that the mishkan is not a building. It is a very large and elaborate tent covered with several layers of wall hangings. The first layer is a woven mixture of dyed wools and linen. The second layer is made of goat hair. These two oversized coverings also cover the outsides of its walls. The very top of the mishkan is further covered by dyed ram skins and tachash hides.[1]

In addition to these beautiful coverings, the mishkan has two sections. The innermost and most important part is called the Holy of Holies. The ark is kept there. The outer chamber is called the "holy chamber." It contains the menorah and the table for the show-bread (as well as the golden altar, which will be described in next week's reading). These two sections are separated by two curtains woven of dyed wools and linen. One is placed between the Holy of Holies and the holy chamber, and the other covers the entrance to the mishkan itself.

1. It is unclear what type of animal the *tachash* actually is. Many believe it was a kind of wild beast that only existed at the time the mishkan was built. It is also thought to have been multicolored.

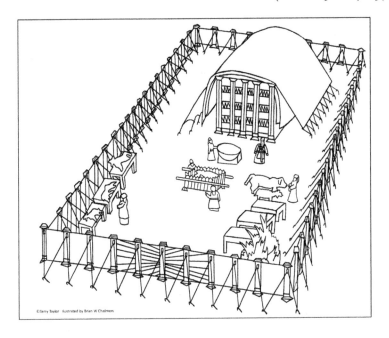

"And let them make Me a sanctuary that I may dwell among them. Exactly as I show you—the pattern of the Tabernacle and the pattern of all its furnishings—so shall you make it."

—Exodus 25:8–9

Life Lessons from *Terumah*

There is a basic challenge when thinking about this week's reading. We believe that each week's reading has life lessons that apply to every generation. However, the focus of our reading this week is God's command to the Jewish people to build a mishkan, and that seems limited to the people who only recently left Egypt. What does it have to do with our lives? Let's take a look and see what life lessons we can discover in the details of building a mishkan.

The Home We Make for God, Part One[2]

If you read through the verses that describe the building of the mishkan, you will notice some similarities with the verses that describe the creation story in the beginning of the book of Genesis. Here are a few examples:

The Universe (Genesis)	The *Mishkan* (Exodus)
And God made the sky	They shall make me a sanctuary
And God made the two large lights	They shall make an ark
And God made the beasts of the earth	Make a table
And God saw all that He had made, and behold it was very good.	Moses saw all the skilled work, and behold they had done it; as God commanded it, they had done it.
The heavens and earth and all of their array were completed.	All the work of the Tabernacle of the tent of meeting was completed.
And God completed all the work that He had done.	And Moses completed the work
And God blessed	And Moses blessed
And sanctified it	And you shall sanctify it and all its vessels

Look closely at the verbs used in both stories: "make," "see," "complete," "bless," "sanctify," and "work." They are the same. What can we learn from this? Just as the universe begins with an act of creation, so, too, does the history of the Jewish people. In a sense, for the Jewish people, making a mishkan is what creating the universe is for God.

There is another notable similarity between the creation story of Genesis and the story of building the mishkan. At the end of the creation story, when Adam and Eve are sent out of the garden of

2. This is another life lesson based on the writings of Rabbi Jonathan Sacks. It comes from an essay entitled "The Home We Make for God" in his commentary on the Pentateuch, *Covenant & Conversation*.

Eden, there are angels, called cherubim, who guard the entrance back into the garden. In the mishkan, at its very center, rests the ark, and on top of this ark are two cherubim.[3]

What is the point of all these clear connections and similarities?

First, it seems clear that the mishkan is meant to serve as a symbol for—and perhaps even a model of—the universe. And just as the Jewish people are commanded to treat the mishkan with great care and respect, we, too, should treat the world we live in with great care and respect. You probably do a lot to show your respect for the world without even being aware of it. Maybe it's through a recycling program at your school or your home. Maybe your family drives an electric or hybrid car. Maybe it's something as simple as never throwing trash out of your car window on your way to school or to a friend's house.

Second, the mishkan is all about the relationship between God and His people. When God first created humans, He had a special relationship with them. But then Adam and Eve disobeyed God's command not to eat from the Tree of Knowledge. By doing so, they damaged that special relationship and had to leave the garden.

But just because the relationship between people and God was damaged does not mean it was not still there. It was, but it had somehow grown smaller and less visible. For example, we know that before they sinned, Adam and Eve could hear "the sound of the LORD God moving about in the garden at the breezy time of day." Outside the garden, they knew that God was there, but He was less visible to them. Their life became what we would call more "normal" and "natural." It was no longer filled with the miracles of living in the Garden of Eden.

God never forgot His special connection with Adam and Eve. We can even say that He wanted it back, and once the Jews left Egypt, God saw an opportunity to restore it. This helps us understand why He commands the Jewish people to "make Me a

3. Rabbi Sacks points out that according to the midrash, the ark contained a Torah scroll. This, too, he says, is a hint to the creation story, because the book of Proverbs describes the Torah as "a tree of life to those who grasp it."

sanctuary that I may dwell among them." He longs to be seen and heard by His people once again.

While we cannot build a mishkan today, this story is telling us that we can and should make a place for God, not only in our homes but inside each of us. When God tells the people who are gathered around Mount Sinai that He wishes to "dwell among them," He is speaking to us, too. The commandment to build a mishkan may have applied only to that specific generation, but making space for God in ourselves and in our lives is not bound by time or place. It is something each of us can do today and always.

Can you think of one thing you did today to create a home for God inside you?

The Home We Make for God, Part Two

If you have studied light in your science class, you have certainly seen how a prism works. If not, here is a simple explanation.

A prism is a piece of glass that has several flat sides, called faces. People use prisms to bend light. This means that when white light is shined through a prism, the light is bent or separated into the different bands of color that make up the rainbow. Without the prism, we can't see all the colors of light. We only see the white light. A prism gives us a new and deeper understanding of what makes up white light.

What does all this have to do with this week's reading?

The Torah is the bright light of God's law given over to humanity. Different scholars and teachers from different times living in different cultures act like prisms. They see the same light of God's law, but their teachings emphasize different aspects of the law. In other words, their insights help us see and appreciate all the colors, so to speak, of God's laws.

One of the very interesting (and some would say unique) ways of examining the stories and laws of the Torah is called *chasidut*. Chasidut embraces the laws and rituals of traditional Judaism. Its followers study the same legal codes and read the same weekly readings from the Torah as do all Jews. But one of the things that makes chasidut different is its willingness to look very carefully at the verses in the Torah for hidden and new meanings. In this way, chasidut is a little like a prism, allowing us to see new "colors" in the verses of the Torah. This week's reading has a great example.

We have already discussed the idea of building a home for God and how each of us can try to do it. Let's take a closer look at the verse that tells us to do this: "Let them make Me a Sanctuary that I may dwell among them." Do you notice anything strange about this verse? If not, take another look. The word "sanctuary" is in the singular, so the verse should have concluded "that I may dwell in it." Instead, the verse uses a plural word, "them." Why the switch from singular to plural?

The most common explanation is that God doesn't merely want to dwell in *it*, that is, in the sanctuary. He wants to live in each of us, as we have already discussed. This is a beautiful thought, but chassidut sees a deeper meaning in this verse.

Most teachers and scholars read this verse as a desire. In other words, God is telling us what He wants. He wants us to make room inside ourselves for Him. Chasidut reads the verse differently. It teaches that this verse isn't just telling us what God wants. It is God making a promise to us. It is as if the verse were saying, If you make room in yourself for God, God is promising that He will dwell inside you.

What's the difference?

If the verse is just telling us what God wants, maybe the "house" we build in ourselves will be good enough, or maybe it won't. But if it's a promise, then no matter how good a "house" we build—a big one or a small one, a beautiful one or a simple one—if we make a place for God, He promises us that He will come and dwell in the place we create for Him.

That is a very powerful lesson, because God is saying, "If you do your part, I promise I will do mine."

> *We already asked you if you can think of things you've done to create a home for God inside yourself. Can you think of things that have made you feel like God has kept His promise and is dwelling inside you?*

Who Really Benefits from Charity

As we have discussed, in this week's reading, God commands the Jewish people to build Him a mishkan. Since the people (and not God!) are to do the actual building, we might have expected God to also command the people to bring the materials needed to construct the mishkan. God actually gives Moses a long list of things needed to build it: gold, silver, and copper; blue, purple, and crimson yarns; fine linen and goat hair; tanned ram skins, *tachash* skins, and acacia wood; oil for lighting; spices for the anointing oil and for the aromatic incense; onyx and other stones for the *ephod* (one of the special garments worn by the priests who served in the mishkan) and for the breastpiece. But the one thing God does *not* do is command the people to bring all these items. He asks them instead, and He tells Moses to accept gifts "from every person whose heart so moves him (or her)."

Why ask instead of command? That's a good question. Let's try to answer it by using a real-life example.

Suppose your school announces a campaign to help needy people in your community. You decide to donate eighteen dollars.[4] You could ask your parents to give you the money, or you could take money from your allowance. You could even sell brownies and lemonade on your street to raise money for the campaign. How you get the money you give doesn't matter to the person getting the money. He or she is simply glad to have money to buy food or clothing or whatever he or she needs. But from your perspective, how you get the money does matter.

The rabbis of the Talmud very much understood the impact that giving charity can have on the giver, and we see this from the Hebrew word they use for charity: *tzedaka*. These rabbis had to come up with a Hebrew word for charity because there is none in the Torah, even though the idea of charity and helping the poor is often discussed. The word *tzedaka* literally means "righteousness" or "justice," and the rabbis' choice of this word teaches us a lot

4. Each Hebrew letter has a numeric equivalent, and the numeric equivalent of the Hebrew word for life, *chai*, is eighteen. This explains why many Jews give charity in multiples of eighteen.

about their attitude toward charity. Their word choice emphasizes the act of giving rather than the act of receiving. Simply put, the rabbis are saying that giving is itself a righteous act. Thinking of charity this way means that the person who receives charity does more for the giver (by letting him or her do a righteous act) than the giver does for the receiver.

How is this supposed to work? The idea is that the person who gives charity learns to be sympathetic and empathetic about the situation of the needy person. The giver learns not to be judgmental. (After all, sometimes things happen that no one can control or predict, and as a result, a person can find himself or herself needing charity.) The giver also becomes more grateful for all the good things in life that he or she has. Finally, the giver becomes more aware of the needs of the community and becomes more active in communal affairs.

In other words, giving charity is a way through which we can become kinder and better people. This can happen if we make the choice, if we decide on our own to do this. Why? Choosing means that we have given it some thought, that we have taken the time to see the needs in our community and then decided to do something to help.

That is the message behind God's asking the people to give what is needed to build the mishkan instead of commanding them to give. Had God commanded the Jewish people to give, they certainly would have, but with little thought. They would have given mechanically.

The same holds true for us. If we are charitable without thinking much about it, our giving still helps the poor and the needy, but it does nothing for us. However, when your heart is inclined to give (as was the case for the Jewish people when building the mishkan), it is a sure sign that you are on the path toward becoming a better person.

Do you or your family have a favorite charity? What do you do to support that charity? How does helping the charity make you feel?

Tetzaveh

(Exod 27:30–30:10)

Sights and Smells

Summary of This Week's Reading

Last week's reading gave us the details of the construction of the mishkan. This week we have additional details about the mishkan. The parasha describes the special garments worn by the priests, including the high priest (the highest ranking of all the priests) when serving in the mishkan, as well as one of the more important structures in the mishkan, the incense altar.

The reading begins with God's command to use the purest of olive oils to light the menorah each day. Next, Moses is told to prepare Aaron and his sons to serve in the mishkan. This involves bringing Aaron and his sons to the door of the mishkan, where they immerse themselves in a special ritual bath and then are dressed in their priestly garments.

Both the high priest and the regular priests are to wear four basic garments: tunics (long-sleeved robes that are both loose-fitting and long enough to reach their ankles); turbans (a type of head covering); sashes (a kind of cloth belt); and pants (worn under the tunics). However, the high priest is to wear some extra very special items.

The first of these is a kind of reversed apron, called an ephod *in Hebrew, with shoulder straps studded with precious stones. This apron is to cover his back.*

Next is the "breastplate of judgment" (choshen mishpat in Hebrew). This cloth breastplate is to have four rows of precious stones, with each row containing three stones. Skilled workmen are to engrave the name of one of the twelve tribes of Israel on each stone. The breastplate will also have a fold that makes a kind of pocket, and this pocket will be used to hold a parchment (called the urim ve-tumim) on which God's name will be written. (While this name can be written, it is considered so holy that it is never said out loud!) Finally, the breastplate will have straps, which will be used to connect it to the ephod.

There are two other items that are to be worn only by the high priest: the me'il and the tzitz. The me'il is a blue robe adorned with golden bells and cloth "pomegranates." The tzitz is a golden band worn on his forehead. On it are engraved the words "Holy to God."

The reading concludes by describing a variety of different sacrifices. Moses offers various sacrifices on behalf of Aaron and his sons to celebrate the beginning of their service in the mishkan. God then commands Moses to repeat this offering for a seven-day period, after which Aaron and his sons are to officially start to work in the mishkan. God also instructs the people to offer two burnt offerings daily: one lamb in the morning and another in the afternoon.

The final offering described in this week's reading involves no animals at all. Rather, the priests are commanded to burn incense (nice smelling spices) on a special incense altar twice daily.

Life Lessons from Tetzaveh

The mishkan was central to the Jewish people's worship during their forty years in the desert. It remained so until the temple was built 480 years after Joshua led the people into Canaan after the death of Moses. And while it has been more than three thousand years since the Jewish people served God in the mishkan, its symbolism is just as important today as it was in the time of Moses.

In this week's reading, we have detailed descriptions of the clothing worn by the priests who served in the mishkan and of the incense altar upon which sweet-smelling spices were burned daily. These, along with the seven-branch menorah we read about last week, have important lessons for us about the good deeds we should do on a regular basis.

The Symbolism of Light

In the creation story in the book of Genesis, God creates in a single instant all the material He uses to build the universe during the next six days.[1] And what is the first thing God puts in place after His initial, all-encompassing act of creation? Light, as the verse tells us: "God said: 'Let there be light; and there was light.' God saw that the light was good, and God separated the light from the darkness."

It seems that the starting point of the universe as we know it is light, and as God Himself says, light is good. Light is meant to drive away and separate us from darkness. We see this idea in movies and fairy tales. We hear this in children's stories. And it is made clear from the design and the construction of the mishkan itself.

At the center of the mishkan were the most special and holy items: the ark that held the tablets Moses brought down from Mount Sinai; the golden table for the show bread; the incense altar (which we will soon discuss); and the menorah. The candles of the menorah were kept burning all day every day. Of course, the light was needed so that the priests who burned the incense or who brought in the showbread could see. But if the purpose of the menorah was simply to light up the space, any sort of candelabra would have worked. There was no need for such an

---

1. The Torah begins with the well-known verse "In the beginning of God's creation of heaven and earth . . ." The Hebrew word for "create" means to create something from nothing, and the sages of the Talmud understood this verse as teaching that God used all the elements and materials He created at that moment to assemble and build the rest of the universe. (Modern scientists think of this moment as the "Big Bang.") If you look carefully at the text, the word "create" is used only two more times: when God creates the Leviathan (whatever that may be) and when He creates the first humans. Everything else—the sun and moon, the oceans and dry land, sea animals and land animals—is either "made" or "formed." It is not "created."

elaborate one or one made (according to the midrash) by God Himself. There must be something more to the menorah than the light that comes from its candles.

There is, and we find an answer from the design of the temple, the permanent structure built by King Solomon to replace the mishkan.[2] In ancient stone buildings like the temple, which had very thick walls, the windows were wide on the outside and narrower on the inside, in a funnel-like shape. This type of window was meant to allow as much light as possible to shine in from the outside to the inside of the building. However, in the inner chamber of the temple, where the menorah and the other holy objects stood, the windows were narrow on the outside and

2. The idea for a temple came from Solomon's father, King David. David thought it was wrong that he lived in a beautiful, fancy palace while God's home among the Jewish people was a tent (even though it was a very special tent). David wanted to build a permanent home for God as beautiful as his palace, and he even began collecting the materials needed to build it. However, David had been a great warrior, and God felt that the temple should not be built by soldiers but instead by men of peace. God told David that he would get credit (so to speak) for the idea of building a temple but that the actual construction would be left to his son Solomon.

wide on the inside—the reverse of the structure of normal windows of the time. This was no accident. This reverse funnel shape was intended to let the light of the menorah shine as much as possible into the outside world.

The windows in the temple were shaped like this.

Solomon understood that the light of the menorah was no ordinary light. It was godly light, and as we read in Genesis, God's light is good. It is meant to help us see clearly, to see what is good in our lives and to steer clear of the bad.

Even today, when all we can do is read about the light of the menorah, this light is still a symbol of good and a call to action. The candles in the menorah were always burning bright, and in a similar manner, we must always strive to be a reflection of this light by doing what is good and just. In this way, we do our part to drive darkness out of the world.

Do you have a favorite book or story about good versus evil? What do you like best about it? Is light used as a symbol for good in this book or story? How?

The Symbolism of Clothing

There's an old saying that "clothes make the man" (or, as we'd say today, "or the woman"). I bet you can think of lots of examples. For instance, the men and women who work for the police and fire departments in their cities are identifiable by the uniforms they wear. The same is true of doctors and nurses, with their white coats and scrubs. And we all know about the special clothes kings and queens wear, from their beautiful robes to their magnificent crowns.

In this week's reading, we have a detailed description of the special clothes the high priest wore whenever he served in the mishkan: the reversed apron with its precious stone-studded shoulder straps that covered his back; the "breastplate of judgment," with its four rows of precious stones; a blue robe with golden bells and cloth "pomegranates"; and a golden band worn on his forehead that was engraved with the words "Holy to God."

This uniform bestowed honor on the high priest who wore it and honor on the God he served. More important, it was meant to be a sign to the man himself that his inside (meaning, his thoughts and actions) should be as beautiful as his outside (symbolized by his special clothing).

What does it mean to be the same on the inside and the outside? Think about it this way: Imagine a child who is very polite and respectful when the family is invited out but who is very rude to Mom and Dad at home. Or how about a classmate who tells everyone how smart he or she is but when there is a test, he or she cheats and copies the answers from others?

When a person acts one way in private and another way in public, we call them a hypocrite. A hypocrite is someone who pretends to be something he or she is not. And this is the life lesson we learn from the special clothing of the high priest.

Any male descendant of Aaron could become the high priest and wear these holy garments. But when the choice was made as to who would actually serve as high priest, the man's character was key. Was he kind? Was he honest? Was he wise and learned? Did his actions at home reflect his actions in public? If not, his wearing the holy garments of the priesthood would make him nothing more than an "empty suit."[3]

> Have you ever known people who acted one way in private and very differently in public? How did that make you feel about them? Would you want to be friends with such a person?

The Symbolism of the Incense

The symbolic items we have discussed so far, the menorah and the clothing of the high priest, are more familiar to most students of the Bible than the incense offering. And truthfully, when there was a mishkan, the menorah and the priestly garments were literally more visible. The menorah was more than five feet tall and made completely of gold.

The priestly garments were beautiful and elegant and inspired awe among the people every time they saw the high priest. As for the incense, it had a pleasing smell, but there was nothing to see. Nonetheless, the incense offering was considered by some to be the most special service in the mishkan. Here's why.

First, the incense was burned not once but twice daily on the golden or "inner" altar that stood within the inner section of the mishkan. (This inner altar was distinct from the outdoor copper altar upon which animal sacrifices were brought.) Second, one of the highlights, if not *the* highlight, of the services performed by the high priest on Yom Kippur (the Day of Atonement on the Jewish calendar) was his entering the Holy of Holies with a pan of smoldering coals in one hand and a ladle filled with incense in the other. He would carefully place this incense over the coals and only leave the Holy of Holies once it was filled with the sweet-smelling smoke of the burning incense.

---

3. Urbandictionary.com defines "an empty suit" as "an insult to disparage others who really don't deserve the title. . . . He or she is ineffectual, perhaps a phony, and is about as relevant or helpful as a suit hanging on a rack."

Today, there is no mishkan, and there are no special Yom Kippur offerings. What, then, does the incense symbolize? What can it teach us?

One possible answer can be found in a story about Abraham from the book of Genesis. After his wife Sarah dies, Abraham takes another wife. Her name is Keturah. It's an unusual name—so unusual that the midrash felt a need to explain its meaning. The name Keturah, says the midrash, sounds very similar to the Hebrew word for incense (*ketoret*), and she was called Keturah because her deeds were as beautiful and sweet as the scent of incense.

Now we can understand why the incense was so important in the mishkan in general and on Yom Kippur specifically. The incense that was burnt on the inner altar reminds us that God sees our good deeds as being as beautiful and sweet as the incense itself. That is why (according to some sages and rabbis) before we do almost anything in life, we should stop and ask ourselves: Will what I am about to do be as pleasing to God as the aroma of the incense? If you can answer yes, you will surely be doing good.

> *Light, clothing, and even sweet smells can be symbols of good. Which of these do you think can be the best reminder to do good? Why?*

Ki Tisa

(Exod 30:11–34:35)

Part One (for Parents and Educators)—A Golden Calf? Really?

This week's reading has the most difficult and challenging story in the entire book of Exodus: the incident of the golden calf. In brief, after God reveals Himself on Mount Sinai and speaks the Ten Utterances in the presence of the whole Jewish people, Moses goes up the mountain to meet with God for forty days and forty nights. While the Pentateuch tells us that Moses and God spoke "face to face," we really don't know what went on during these forty days.[1] But there is one thing that we do know for sure: the people (or a group of people) built an idol of gold and worshipped it before Moses returned to the camp. Here is how the Torah describes the scene:

> *When the people saw that Moses was so long in coming down from the mountain, the people gathered against Aaron and said to him, "Come, make us a god who shall go before us, for that man Moses, who brought us from the land of Egypt—we do not know what has happened to him." Aaron said to them, "Take off the gold rings that are on the ears of your wives, your sons, and your daughters, and bring them to me." And all the people took off the gold rings that were in their ears and brought them to Aaron.*

1. The midrash, of course, offers many stories and insights on what goes on between Moses and God, but that is not our focus here.

> *This he took from them and cast in a mold, and made it into a molten calf. And they exclaimed, "This is your god, O Israel, who brought you out of the land of Egypt!" When Aaron saw this, he built an altar before it; and Aaron announced: "Tomorrow shall be a festival of the LORD!" Early the next day, the people offered up burnt offerings and brought sacrifices of well-being; they sat down to eat and drink, and then rose to dance.*

It's hard to know where to begin trying to make sense of this story. How can a people who witnessed the plagues in Egypt, experienced the splitting of Yam Suf, and heard the voice of God as they stood at Mount Sinai make and worship a calf of gold? The scholars and rabbis who comment on this story give several explanations to try to make this story understandable.

The first question these commentators address is, What exactly were the people doing?

This question is discussed in an interesting midrash. According to this midrash, Moses tells the people he will return from Mount Sinai in forty days. Seems pretty simple, right? Or maybe not. Let's say a friend says to you on Monday that you will have a play date in two days. Is Monday part of the count? If so, your play date will be on Tuesday. If not, it will be on Wednesday. This example reminds us that we need to be very clear in such matters. But Moses is not so clear. He has in mind that he will return at the *end* of the fortieth day, that is, late in the afternoon. The people, it seems, have a different way of counting. They think that the fortieth day means the beginning of the day, not its end. So, early on day forty, they begin waiting for Moses to return. One hour passes. Then two, then three. Soon it is noon, and no Moses. At this point, the people believe that Moses is never coming back. They become very worried, even scared. How are they to communicate with God without Moses? How will they know what God wants them to do?

Why would they be concerned about this? Just look at their experiences in Egypt and at Mount Sinai. Moses brought the word of God to Pharaoh. Moses taught the Jewish people God's laws at Mount Sinai. It is understandable for the people to believe that they need Moses (or someone like Moses) to represent them before God. They were sure that they could not communicate directly to God, and so, they decided to "make" a new Moses.

What does it mean to "make" a new Moses? According to one understanding of this story, the people merely wanted a new leader in place of Moses, not a new god.[2] In other words, they didn't see themselves as worshipping the golden calf as an alternative to God. They somehow believed that this idol could represent them before God, just as Moses had done before he disappeared.[3]

The second point addressed by the commentators is, Who exactly worshipped the golden calf?

At first glance, this seems like a silly question, because the text clearly says that "all the people took off the gold rings that were in their ears and brought them to Aaron . . . . And they exclaimed [when they saw the golden calf], 'This is your god, O Israel, who brought you out of the land of Egypt!'" The midrash, however, points to a different part of the story, where God says to Moses, "Hurry down, for your people, whom you brought out of the land of Egypt, have acted basely." The midrash notes that God does not say "the people" but instead tells Moses that "your people" are sinning. And who are these people? They are "the mixed multitude," that is, a group of around three thousand Egyptians and people of other nationalities who wished to leave Egypt with the Jews and worship their God. Moses brought them along without consulting God, and now, when Moses seems to have disappeared, they quickly go back to idol worship.

The problem with this explanation is that the story reads as if all the people were worshipping the golden calf. If only three

2. See Nachmanides on Exod 32:2.

3. Why they did not turn to Aaron is unclear, and it is equally uncertain why they chose the form of a calf for their golden idol. Perhaps it was because they had lived in Egypt, where people had worshipped idols, for hundreds of years. Or maybe it was simply because, as historians tell us, the bull had an important role in the art and religious texts of the ancient Near East. (For example, Hadad, the Semitic god of storms, thunder, and rain, is often depicted standing on a bull.)

thousand actually committed this sinful act, why does the story mention "all the people?" The answer is simple.

In next week's reading, we will see that Moses takes a census, or a count, of the adult men who are of military age (that is, between the ages of twenty and sixty). There were more than six hundred thousand men in this age group. Add to this the women, children, and older men and there were approximately two to three million people who left Egypt with Moses. Now, imagine that three thousand people start worshipping an idol. Were there not hundreds of thousands of other people who could have stopped them? Of course there were, but they didn't. And because they didn't, the story reads as if "all the people" sinned.

This explanation makes more sense, and it has the additional benefit of teaching us an important lesson. When people stand by and do nothing to stop wrongdoing, it is as if they took part in the wrongdoing. Standing by passively in the face of terrible or sinful actions is just unacceptable.

There is one final point worth noting, and it is true whether all the people or only some of the people worshipped the golden calf. The starting point for both is that this story makes no sense. How could the Jewish people possibly worship an idol a mere forty days after receiving God's laws at Mount Sinai? This is why scholars and rabbis alike tend to reject the idea that the Jews actually worshipped an idol and struggle to find an alternative explanation.

Maybe the explanations offered here for this difficult story make sense to you. Maybe they don't. But even if you are left with more questions than answers, that does not mean that you should skip this story. Not understanding something is no reason for not trying to figure it out, especially when it comes to the Bible.

Ki Tisa

(Exod 30:11–34:35)

Part Two—More on the Mishkan

Summary of This Week's Reading

The Jewish people remain camped at the base of Mount Sinai, but their thoughts must certainly be turning toward the land of Canaan, which will be their new home. (Remember, at this point in the story, God has not yet decided that the people will spend forty years in the desert.) Conquering the land, even with God's help, will require an army, and to create an army, Moses needs to know how many men there are who can serve in the army. This is likely why God tells Moses at the beginning of this week's reading to take a census, or count, of the adult males between the ages of twenty and sixty. But for reasons that are not so clear, God tells Moses that he cannot count the people directly. He must instead collect a special silver coin, called a half shekel, from each individual. These coins will be melted down and made into sockets for the beams of the mishkan.

God next gives Moses a series of instructions having to do with different aspects of the mishkan. God tells Moses to make a copper washstand, which will be used by the priests to wash their hands and feet before they go to work in the mishkan. God gives Moses the recipe for making holy "anointing oil," which is to be used to anoint the mishkan and its vessels as well as Aaron and his sons. ("Anointing" means rubbing or pouring oil on something or someone, and this action is used to show how special and holy these items and men were.) God also gives Moses the formula for the incense that is to be offered twice each day in the mishkan.

Moses has the instructions, but he still needs workers to do the actual building of the mishkan. Bezalel now makes his entrance, having been given great wisdom by God Himself. God instructs Moses to put Bezalel in charge of building the mishkan and making everything that will be used in it. God also appoints Oholiab as Bezalel's assistant.

At this point, the story takes a sharp turn. God tells the Jewish people to observe the Sabbath, saying that the Sabbath will be the eternal sign between Him and the people.[1] This concludes the discussion of the mishkan, and our reading introduces a new topic.

After the revelation and giving of the Ten Utterances at Mount Sinai, God calls to Moses and tells him to go up the mountain, where he will spend forty days and forty nights. (There are no details about this meeting between God and Moses, but Jewish tradition says that Moses learned all God's laws during this time and was given two stone tablets upon which God carved the Ten Utterances.) Before he leaves, Moses tells the people he will be gone for forty days, but somehow, the people miscount the days.[2] When Moses does not come back when the people believe he is supposed to return, they become scared and impatient.

At this point in the story, we need to look to the midrash for more details, because the text itself does not give us many. The text states that "the people gathered against Aaron," which suggests that they are prepared to hurt him (maybe even kill him) if he does not "make us a god who shall go before us." It then says that Aaron cast a mold and made a "molten calf."

---

1. Most rabbis and scholars see a crucial connection between the building of the mishkan and the command to observe the Sabbath. By telling the people to observe the Sabbath immediately after He gives them instructions about how to build the mishkan, God makes it clear that no work on the mishkan should be done on the Sabbath. In other words, even something as important as building the mishkan must be set aside on the Sabbath day.

2. As we have already discussed, Moses had in mind that he would return at the *end* of the fortieth day, that is, late in the afternoon. The people thought that the fortieth day meant at the beginning of the day and not at its end.

Did Aaron really agree so quickly to their demands? Did he really do nothing to stop them?

According to the midrash, Aaron knows that what the people are asking is wrong, but as the text suggests, the people were threatening to hurt him if he didn't cooperate. What does Aaron do in the midrash's version of the story? He pretends to agree and tries to delay things as much as possible, because he knows exactly when Moses will return. This is why when the people gather against him, he tells the men to ask their wives to donate their gold jewelry. Aaron knows the women will say no, and he hopes that will delay matters.

But things go badly. The men don't ask. They take the gold from their wives, and thus, despite Aaron's best efforts, a god of gold, in the form of a golden calf, is made, and the next morning people begin to dance around this idol and offer sacrifices to it.

God, of course, gets very angry. He seems prepared to destroy the people and start fresh. Moses begs God to reconsider and to forgive the people. God agrees and sends Moses down the mountain with the two stone tablets.

Moses thinks he is prepared for the worst, but he's not. When he sees people dancing around the idol, he becomes so angry that he breaks the tablets given to him by God. Moses understands that he must stop these sinful acts and punish those who seem to be worshipping this golden idol.

Moses is part of the tribe of Levi, and he trusts his fellow tribesmen. He asks for their help, and they agree. Together with Moses, they execute three thousand people who worshipped the golden calf.

This is a tragic story to be sure, and Moses is worried that God has not fully forgiven the people. So Moses goes back up the mountain, for another forty days and forty nights, to beg and plead with God. God hears Moses's prayers. He tells Moses to go back down and lead the Jews toward the promised land, the land of Canaan. But God is still disturbed enough that He tells Moses He will no longer personally lead the people on their journey. Instead, God will send an angel to lead the way. God also sends a plague upon the people, killing thousands more.

God's displeasure with the Jews is obvious to Moses, and he therefore takes action on his own, moving his tent away from the main camp.[3] Despite this, Moses begs and pleads some more. He asks God to reconsider having an angel lead them. God hears Moses's pleas and agrees to lead them Himself.

Moses has one last request for God. He asks God: "Let me behold Your Presence!" It is unclear what Moses means by this or what he hopes to see. After all, Moses has just spent a total of eighty days with God, interacting and speaking with God, as the verse says, "face to face."

In response to this request, God tells Moses that "you cannot see My face, for man may not see Me and live." God does allow Moses to see His back (again, we have no idea what this really means), but God again tells Moses: "My face must not be seen."

When these "negotiations" are complete, God tells Moses to carve new tablets upon which God will engrave the Ten Utterances. Moses takes the new, blank tablets up to Mount Sinai. There, God seals a covenant (which is a very special kind of agreement) with Moses and assures him again that God's presence will dwell with the Jews.

---

3. Even though Moses moved his tent outside the main camp, the people still come and stand by his tent to ask him questions. The text describes the scene: "When Moses entered the Tent, the pillar of cloud would descend and stand at the entrance of the Tent, while [God] spoke with Moses. When all the people saw the pillar of cloud poised at the entrance of the Tent, all the people would rise and bow low, each at the entrance of his tent."

*God then informs the Jewish people that He will drive the Ca-
naanites out of the land. He instructs the Jews to destroy all forms
of idolatry in Canaan and tells them not to make any treaties with
the people who might still be living there. God also gives the Jews a
series of commandments, which include the commandment not to
eat any leavened foods (like bread and crackers) on Passover and
not to cook meat together with milk.*

*This week's reading concludes by telling us of Moses's changed
appearance once he comes down from Mount Sinai. Moses doesn't
realize it, but beams of light shine off his face. This frightens the
people (understandably). To calm the people, Moses wears a veil on
his face, but he removes it when speaking to God or when he repeats
God's words to the people.*

Life Lessons from *Ki Tisa*

This week's reading gives us additional details about the construction of the mishkan. But just because it is once again discussing the
same topic (the mishkan) does not mean that it is lacking in important commandments and stories that have great meaning even in
our days. Let's see what life lessons they have to offer us.

Same but Different

Coins are often used in interesting ways when we study the Torah and try to understand its deeper meaning. For example, when
examining how unique and different people can be, the midrash
uses the metaphor of a coin.[4] The midrash compares a person who
mints coins to God. When coins were made in ancient times, they
were stamped using a seal. Using the same seal over and over again
would make identical coins. This made sense. Coins are supposed
to be the same. Even today, everyone knows what a penny looks
like. The same is true of nickels, dimes, and quarters. Each kind of
coin looks like all others of the same type.

---

4. Tosefta 8:5, cited in the Babylonian Talmud Sanhedrin 38a.

The midrash goes on to say that God, like a minter of coins, uses a single seal (what we would today call a "template") when He creates people. What is this template God uses? The first humans, of course: Adam and Eve. However, even though God uses the same template over and over, everyone is different. People may be similar, but, unlike coins, each is unique, with his or her own strengths and character traits.

This week's reading contains another important story involving coins and what coins can symbolize. Moses is commanded to take a census of the people, but God tells him not to actually count the people. Instead, Moses is to collect a special coin—a half-shekel—from each person. And the verse is very clear about this: "The rich shall not pay more and the poor shall not pay less than half a shekel when giving the LORD's offering."

Limiting the donation of each person to a half-shekel coin is a little strange. These coins were used to pay for the construction of the mishkan. Would it not have been better and more practical to let the rich people give more so that there would be even more money available? Perhaps, but by limiting each person's gift to a half-shekel, God is telling the Jewish people something very noteworthy. Since everyone gives the same coin, no one can say that he or she is more important than anyone else because of how much money he or she gave to build the mishkan. In other words, with the command to give the same coin, God is showing the people that the rich and the poor have equal value in His eyes. He wants the people to understand that He loves and watches over each person without checking their wallet or bank account.

Think about how different our world would be if people looked at each other as God looks at us!

> When choosing friends, do you look for people who are exactly *like you* (that is, they enjoy the same music, movies, clothes, and so on)? Or do you look for friends who are a little different from you? When choosing your friends, what qualities are most important? Which ones really don't matter?

To Act or Not to Act

We have already discussed the story of the golden calf and the failure of the people to stop the small group of individuals who built and worshipped it. Let's see what history and the Torah have to say about the question of whether or not to act when confronted with wrongdoing or, worse still, evil.

In the 1930s and 1940s, Hitler and his Nazi party did terrible things to groups of people across Europe who were different from them, and no group suffered more than the Jews. Six million Jews were murdered in twenty-two different countries by the Nazis in something called the Holocaust (the *Shoah* in Hebrew). Hitler made no secret of what he planned to do to the Jews of Germany and all of Europe when he became the head of the German government in 1933. Yet, most Germans remained silent. They did little to stand up to the Nazis.

Something similar happened in America during the 1950s and 1960s. People weren't killed like they were in Nazi Germany, but bad things were going on across the country. Countless numbers of African Americans were denied things that white people took for granted: things like the right to vote or to go to any school they wanted or just to walk into any restaurant and order a meal. There were many Americans, Black and white alike, who tried to stop these wrongs. However, most Americans stood by silently. They could not bring themselves to act.[5]

The effort to give Blacks and whites the same rights was called the civil rights movement. Its most important leader, Dr. Martin Luther King Jr., summed up the frustrations of the Black community in the face of inaction by their white brothers and sisters: "He who passively accepts evil is as much involved in it as he who helps

5. Interestingly, of the white volunteers who traveled to the South to assist the civil rights movement during the Freedom Rides of 1963 and Freedom Summer of 1964, an estimated 50 percent were Jewish. What prompted this high rate of Jewish participation is unclear, but it certainly reflects Judaism's strong emphasis on social justice, as well as the long history of persecution suffered by Jews around the world over the centuries.

to perpetrate it. He who accepts evil without protesting against it is really cooperating with it."

Dr. King's message is a simple one. If you see something bad happening but do nothing to stop it with either words or actions, it is as if you were taking part in that very action. This is the same lesson we learned from the story of the golden calf. In fact, we might even say that the story of the golden calf and the punishment the people received for doing nothing to stop this terrible wrong could have been a guiding lesson in both Germany and in America. But it wasn't.

The rabbis of the Talmud looked to this story (and to other sections of the Bible as well) as an important reminder for all times. They tell us that when we see someone doing something wrong, we have an obligation to speak up. We must tell that person that what he or she is about to do (or is already doing) is wrong. And what if they don't listen to us? The rabbis say that we must try and try again, even up to a hundred times, to stop them from doing wrong.

Perhaps this is what Moses has in mind when, in his farewell speech to the Jewish people shortly before his death, he tells them, "Justice, justice shall you pursue." Pursuing justice means standing up for what is right. It also means protecting those who are different when they are mistreated simply because they are different. Black or white, Jew or gentile—God uses the same template to create us all. If He is ready to watch over us all, we should do no less.

> It's never easy to confront people and tell them that they are doing something wrong. (This is true whether the person is being a bully or is a good friend doing something that just makes you uncomfortable.) Does this make it okay to remain silent? Or must you tell them (or even yell at them) to stop? Could you tell someone at home about this? At school? At your church or synagogue?

Vayakhel

(Exod 35:1–38:20)

One More Time

Summary of This Week's Reading

This week's reading opens on the day after Moses comes down from Mount Sinai with a second set of stone tablets engraved with the words of the Ten Utterances. (Remember that he broke the first set when he saw people dancing around the golden calf.) In the future, the day of his return will be observed by the Jewish people each year as Yom Kippur, the Day of Atonement.

Now that Moses is back in the camp, what does he do? He gathers all the people together. He of course lets them know that God has forgiven them for the sin of the golden calf. He also lets them know how much God wants the Jewish people to build the mishkan. However, before Moses describes all the materials he needs to build the mishkan, he gives the people a brief reminder about observing the Sabbath. He does this so that the people understand how important the Sabbath is and to let them know that even though God is anxiously awaiting the completion of the mishkan, the people must never work to build it on the Sabbath.

Hearing Moses speak, the people are motivated to donate all the materials needed to construct the mishkan. Moses then announces God's choice of who should be in charge of the construction project: Bezalel and Oholiab. Moses transfers all the donated materials to them, and it seems that it is time for the project to begin. However, the people keep donating more and more materials for the project. This prompts Bezalel to tell Moses that he has more than enough to complete the task. Moses then asks the people to please stop their donations.

Once the actual construction begins, Bezalel and his team start making the wall hangings that will be used to cover the mishkan. They next construct wall panels and weave special curtains to cover the entrance to the mishkan itself as well as a curtain to separate the holy of holies from the rest of the mishkan.

At this point, it is time to build the holy vessels used in the mishkan: the ark, the showbread table, the menorah, and the incense altar. The anointing oil and the incense are also prepared.

The last things to be built by Bezalel and his team are the outer altar (on which animal sacrifices are to be made), the copper wash stand, the mesh curtains that will surround the tabernacle court-yard, and the beams and hooks that hold them in place.

Life Lessons from *Vayakhel*

As we mentioned before, the last five weekly readings in the book of Exodus largely focus on the building of the mishkan, including all vessels used there (like the menorah and the incense altar), as well as the priestly garments. This means that there's not a lot of new material in this week's reading. Nonetheless, it opens with an important reminder.

Judaism believes in a God who is just and fair, and Jews of all denominations understand that He is ready to give out consequences to people who act inappropriately. However, they also know that God's desire for justice is softened by His merciful nature. How far does God's mercy extend? The beginning of this week's reading gives us a good answer to this question.

Moses returns to the camp after spending forty days and nights pleading with God to forgive the people's sin with the golden calf. Were God focused only on strict justice and harsh consequences, He would have ignored Moses's pleas. The fact that He forgives the people, as Moses tells them as soon as he comes down from Mount

Sinai, reminds us how great God's mercy is. This is something worth remembering and reflecting on every day.

Didn't You Already Tell Me That?

"Did you clean up your room?"

"Did you clean up your room?" (A second time.)

"Have you starting cleaning your room yet?" (Okay, the words are a little different, but now it's a third time.)

Even if you haven't starting cleaning your room yet, it can still be a little annoying to hear the same thing over and over again. Why is it, do you think, that your parents (and teachers) so often repeat themselves when asking you to do something?

Here's one possible answer, and it is one we see in the repetition of the details about building the mishkan that are a central part of the book of Exodus.

There are many jobs that require people to make presentations, teach certain facts, or share specific information. These jobs require a great deal of talking and explaining. (There are lots of examples of jobs like this, including being a teacher, lawyer, banker, or salesperson.) Being a good speaker, a successful speaker, can be hard. It can take many years of practice and experience to achieve this. But all good speakers have something in common, which is that they tend to follow three simple rules:

1. Tell your audience in your introduction what you are about to discuss.

2. Talk about it with the audience.

3. Review what you just told them.

That's right. Really good speakers deliver their message to their audience three times. Why? Because good speakers understand (and have probably learned from experience) that the first time people hear something, they rarely "get it." They may not get it the second time, either. But by the third time, the message will have sunk in.

Seen in this light, we can better understand all the repetition involving the building of the mishkan. It's not that God doesn't trust the people. It's not that He thinks they aren't smart enough to understand the hows and whys of building the mishkan. It's simply that God knows that people need to hear something more than once to fully grasp it.

This should by no means be an excuse for you to ignore your parents the first time they ask you to do something! Think of it instead as their way of indicating to you how important something is when they say it a second and third time.

How do you feel when you have to tell someone something more than once?

Modeling Proper Behavior

By now, it should be clear that the Torah is no ordinary book. It tells the history of the Jewish people, but it is not a history book. It contains wonderful stories, but it is not a story book. It has many, many laws and commandments, but it is not just a law book. It is unique in that it is all of this and more.

The special character of the Torah means that nothing in it is there by chance. Every story, every bit of history, is meant to teach us a lesson that we can apply to our daily lives. This week's reading gives us a good example.

After Moses gathers the people together and shares with them how much God is looking forward to their building the mishkan, the people enthusiastically donate the materials needed for this project. Not just some of the people, but all the people, a fact that is emphasized over and over in this story. The verse uses terms like "everyone," "all the skilled workers," and "all the women." The people give so much gold, silver, and copper and so many blue, purple, and crimson yarns and animal skins that Moses has to ask them to stop.

What is most important about this story is its description of what motivates the people to give so much: "all whose hearts moved them." This description makes clear that the people were not commanded to give to the building of the mishkan. They gave because they wanted to give. And that is why the story gives us so many details about what they gave.

The giving in this story is meant to be an example for future generations of how they should respond when their communities are in need. The Torah thus includes it to inspire us to act in a similar way when the opportunity or need arises.

> *Giving to a charity may not just be about money. What else can you give "when your heart moves you"? How often do you give? Is it something you want to do or just something your parents or teachers tell you that you should do?*

Pekudei

(Exod 38:21–40:38)

At Last, Ready to Use

Summary of This Week's Reading

Once again, our reading is about the mishkan, only now, the actual construction is complete. As a kind of summary, we are given an exact accounting of how much gold, silver, and copper were donated to build the mishkan itself, as well as all the vessels used in it.

There are, however, a few last items to complete. The high priest's ephod—the reversed apron that covers his back—and its precious stone-studded shoulder straps have to be made. So, too, must his "breastplate of judgment," with its four rows of precious stones, each row containing three stones. Once it is complete, skilled craftspeople engrave the names of the twelve tribes of Israel on the stones. They then connect the breastplate to the ephod.

Other workers complete the rest of the priestly garments, and with this, the mishkan and all its vessels are ready to be used. Moses inspects all of this one last time. When he sees that the work has been done exactly as God commanded, Moses blesses the workers.

It is now time to set up the mishkan. God tells Moses to do this on the first day of the Hebrew month of Nisan. (It is no coincidence that this is the same month that the Jewish people left Egypt.) God also tells Moses to put all the vessels in their proper places and to anoint all of them with oil. (This is meant to indicate how very special each of the vessels is.) Finally, Moses is told to dress Aaron and his sons in their priestly garments and to anoint them with oil, too.

Once Moses has done all that God commands him, a "cloud of glory" fills the mishkan. This cloud is a sign that God's presence is resting among the Jewish people. It also serves as a guide throughout the people's travels through the desert. When it lifts, the people travel, following the cloud until it rests. At that spot, they set up camp until the cloud moves again.

Life Lessons from *Pekudei*

After five weekly readings, the telling of the building of the mishkan draws to a close. But for all the repetition and detail in the story, there are still a few important life lessons for us to uncover in this week's reading.

One Last Example of Humility

Moses may have set up the mishkan on the first day of the Hebrew month of Nisan, but it was not really ready to be used. That would only happen eight days later, when Aaron and his sons are officially allowed to work in the mishkan and to perform all the services done there each day. For some reason, that story is only told in the next book of the Torah, the book of Leviticus. Still, it is worth taking a sneak peek at that story, because it teaches us something very important about Aaron.

Aaron has been at Moses's side throughout the entire book of Exodus. He goes with Moses to confront Pharaoh, and he acts as Moses's spokesperson. (Remember that Moses told God when he was first selected to lead the Jewish people that he was "slow of speech and slow of tongue.") Aaron even performs the first three plagues: turning the Nile to blood, bringing swarms of frogs from the Nile, and causing lice to appear on all the Egyptians. And, of course, Aaron is selected to serve as the high priest, and only his descendants can hold this position.

All the same, we cannot ignore the fact that Aaron is the older brother and that his baby brother, Moses, is the great leader. Yet, Aaron is never jealous of Moses or of the special relationship Moses has with God. Why? Because in his own way, Aaron is as humble a person as his brother Moses. And according to the midrash, it is Aaron's humility that made him worthy of being the high priest.

On the day that Aaron is to begin his service as high priest, he hesitates, which prompts Moses to approach him and encourage him: "Approach the altar and perform the services as God has commanded."

Still, Aaron is reluctant to step forward. According to the midrash, he remembers his part in the sin of the golden calf. He is ashamed. He is even afraid to approach the altar to perform the sacrifices because of this sin. Seeing this, Moses says something quite amazing: "Why are you ashamed? It was for this that you were chosen."

With these few words, Moses turns Aaron around. But why? How do these words make Aaron feel less embarrassed or change what Aaron did with the golden calf?

The most common answer given is that it is precisely because of Aaron's feelings of fear and embarrassment that he was chosen. Aaron's broken heart about his past actions shows that he does not think himself worthy of the honor of serving as high priest. In his mind, being Moses's brother, his confidant, and his assistant for so long counts for nothing. Aaron feels he is entitled to nothing, which is the mark of a truly humble person.

A second answer can be found in a famous chasidic story:

> R. Yitzchak Blazer [later known as R. Itzele Peterburger] was pushed by R. Yisrael Salanter to St. Petersburg to accept the major Rabbinic position in Czarist Russia. To put it mildly, St. Petersburg was not Vilna. R. Itzele was therefore extremely hesitant and protested that as a young man, he did not feel ready for the position. R. Yisrael responded: "and whom should I recommend— someone who feels that he is ready?"[1]

---

1. See Brander, "Shemini."

Think about it for a moment. Could anyone really have been ready to serve as the first high priest in God's sanctuary? Of course not, and only someone with a huge ego would believe that he could perform those priestly duties. Aaron, with his true and deep sense of humility, sincerely felt he was not the right person for the task (just as his brother Moses had felt, years before, that he was not the right person to lead the Jewish people out of Egypt).

It was his humility that made Aaron so right for the task, and that is what prompts his brother Moses to say to him: "It was for this [your deep humility] that you were chosen."

> *Thinking you'd be good at something without ever having tried it might be arrogant. But what if you practice a lot and then become good it? Can you still be humble about the skills you worked hard to develop?*

Finishing Where We Began

We began this book with a discussion of the importance of asking questions, so it seems appropriate to revisit this topic as we reach its conclusion.

In this week's reading, we find the phrase "as the LORD had commanded Moses" repeated eighteen times. Why? Is there any reason to think the people would not have followed God's commands when building the mishkan? Of course not! But it is possible to learn something from this about how and when to ask questions.

Moses was very careful to repeat God's instructions about the mishkan many times, so the people really had little need to ask questions. Perhaps there was the occasional "How do I do this" type of question, but probably no questions like "Why are the planks in the walls of the mishkan ten cubits long?" or "Why did the courtyard surrounding the mishkan measure one hundred by fifty cubits?"[2] The simple answer to such questions is, well, just because (as we discussed early in this book).

2. There is some dispute in the Jewish legal codes regarding the exact size of a cubit. The range usually given is from 1.57 to 2.1 feet in length.

This does not mean, however, that the people would not have asked Moses different types of questions. Maybe they asked him about the symbolism of having seven lights in the menorah. (Remember that we, too, have talked about the symbolism of light.) Perhaps they were curious about what could be learned from the fact that communal sacrifices were offered each morning and each afternoon. One can ask many valuable questions without questioning the command of God.

More important, Jewish tradition tells us that Moses taught the laws of God to the people throughout the forty years they wandered in the wilderness before reaching the land of Canaan. The people certainly must have had lots of questions for Moses, because, as we all know, asking questions always helps us learn better.

To better understand this idea, let's look at some examples of questions the people in the wilderness must have asked and that people still ask today.

The Torah is very clear that one may not light a fire on the Sabbath. But what if one lit the fire before the start of the Sabbath? Can the fire continue to burn, or must it be extinguished before sunset?[3] Over the centuries, as people used candles and gas or oil lamps to light their homes, more questions were asked. Can I use the first candle to light other candles on the Sabbath? Can I adjust the flame on the Sabbath? Can I add oil to the lamp on the Sabbath?[4] (In case you missed them, the footnotes below answer all these questions.)

With the discovery of electricity came many more questions. Is a lightbulb a form of fire? Can I use lightbulbs on the Sabbath? If I can use them, can I turn them off and on during the Sabbath?[5]

3. According to Jewish law, one may light a fire before the start of the Sabbath and let it continue to burn.

4. The answer to all three questions is no.

5. In the early days of electricity, there were some Jewish legal experts who thought that light bulbs were like fire because of the heat generated by the filament. As they came to better understand how electricity and lightbulbs work, most Jewish law authorities concluded that light bulbs are not a form of fire as defined by the Torah. Nonetheless, for a variety of legal and social reasons, Orthodox Jews do not use electricity on the Sabbath. Lights may be used on

What do we see from this? Even a verse that seems perfectly clear—"You shall kindle no fire throughout your settlements on the Sabbath day"—can cause people to ask many serious questions.

Cooking is another good example.

In the time of Moses, cooking was usually done over an open flame. Thus, when the Torah states that one may not cook on the Sabbath, it means that one may not cook over an open flame. Once the people conquered the land of Canaan and built permanent settlements, they surely built ovens of some kind. Putting food in the oven would still be cooking over an open flame, but what about on top of the oven? Can one cook food on top of an oven on the Sabbath?[6] What if the food is cooked before the Sabbath? Can one put it in or on the oven during the Sabbath to warm it?[7]

Modern technology led to further complications. When microwave ovens first appeared in homes, many Jewish scholars asked whether microwave cooking met the Torah's definition of cooking. This may not have been a concern in terms of Sabbath observance, because no one would turn on a microwave on the Sabbath. However, this question—whether microwaving is cooking as defined by Jewish law—was of critical importance for the observance of Jewish dietary laws.[8]

The point should be clear. To fully understand and observe God's laws, we must always ask questions. Questions mean that we

---

the Sabbath only if they are controlled by timers that are set before the start of the Sabbath.

6. No, not even if the fire in the oven was kindled before the start of the Sabbath.

7. The simple answer is no. However, the laws of warming already cooked food on the Sabbath are very complex. For example, a hot plate may be used, but using an oven, especially one without a Sabbath setting, is problematic. These laws require careful study and are beyond the scope of our discussion.

8. Many authorities initially did not consider microwaving food to be a form of cooking as defined by the Torah. Today, as microwaves have become a staple of most kitchens, their use is universally held to be cooking per the definitions of Jewish law.

are thinking carefully and seriously about these laws. Questions mean that we are less likely to make mistakes.

And maybe the only way we can truly observe the laws "as the LORD had commanded Moses" is by never being afraid to ask questions.

What are some reasons people ask questions? What kinds of questions would you ask your parents? Your teacher? Your friends?

Sometimes we ask questions just to let someone know we care. A good example is "How are you today?" Can you think of two more questions you could ask your parents or your friends that show you care about them?

Bibliography

Brander, Asher. "Shemini: The Winding Road to Greatness." Website of the Orthodox Union, August 8, 2010. https://www.ou.org/life/torah/shemini_ brander_5769/.

Feiler, Bruce. *America's Prophet: How the Story of Moses Shaped America*. New York: HarperCollins, 2009.

Feldman, Emanuel. "The Odd and Instructive Habits of Non-Observant Jews: A Look at Berit Milah and Pesah." *Tradition: A Journal of Orthodox Jewish Thought* 66, no. 2 (2008) 127–37.

Freund, Michael. "How the Exodus Story Created America." *The Jerusalem Post*, March 29, 2013. https://www.michaelfreund.org/13124/exodus-america.

Ijaz, Saroop. "Pakistan Should Not Again Fail 'Honor Killing' Victim. Human Rights Watch, August 22, 2019. https://www.hrw.org/news/2019/08/22/ pakistan-should-not-again-fail-honor-killing-victim.

Kay, Judith W. "The Exodus and Racism: Paradoxes for Jewish Liberation." *Journal of the Society of Christian Ethics* 28, no. 2 (2008) 5.

Kinnaird, Brian A. "Moses and the Man of Steel: From the Burning Bush to a Burning Building, there's Always a Call for Help!" *Psychology Today*, September 28, 2014. https://www.psychologytoday.com/us/blog/the-hero -in-you/201409/moses-and-the-man-steel.

Nahmanides (Ramban). *The Disputation at Barcelona*. Translated by Charles Ber Chavel. New York: Shilo, 1983.

Raboteau, Albert J. *A Fire in the Bones: Reflections on African-American Religious History*. Boston: Beacon, 1995.

Sacks, Jonathan. "The Home We Make for God." In *Covenant & Conversation: Exodus: The Book of Redemption*, 199–206. New Milford, CT: Maggid, 2010.

Zehavi, Ben. "19th-cent. Slave Bible that Removed Exodus Story to Repress Hope Goes on Display." *The Times of Israel*, March 2019. https://www. timesofisrael.com/19th-cent-slave-bible-that-removed-exodus-story-to-repress-hope-goes-on-display/.

About the Author

Rabbi Reuven Travis earned his bachelor's degree from Dartmouth College, where he graduated Phi Beta Kappa with a double major in French literature and political science. He holds a master's degree in teaching from Mercer University and also earned a master's in Judaic studies from Spertus College. He received his rabbinic ordination from Rabbi Michael J. Broyde, dean of the Atlanta Torah MiTzion Kollel, after spending four years studying with Rabbi Broyde and the members of the kollel.

Rabbi Travis worked in Jewish day schools for 20 years and taught students from second grade through high school. He has previously published three scholarly works on the book of Job, the book of Numbers, and the book of Genesis, respectively, and is currently working on a number of new book projects. He also teaches online classes on topics ranging from the Bible to Jewish medical ethics to American history.

CPSIA information can be obtained
at www.ICGtesting.com
Printed in the USA
LVHW020323070921
697165LV00003B/49